The Animals In Our Lives

The Animals In Our Lives

Stories of
Companionship and Awe

Compiled by

Catherine Lawton

CLADACH
Publishing

THE ANIMALS IN OUR LIVES
STORIES OF COMPANIONSHIP AND AWE
© 2021 by Catherine Lawton

Published by CLADACH Publishing
PO Box 336144 Greeley, CO 80633
https://cladach.com

Cover Photo: © Can Stock Photo / Gajus

ISBN: 9781945099274
Library of Congress Control Number: 2021943023
Printed in the United States of America

"Genuine love for God spills over into loving compassion for all his creatures."

–Elizabeth Theokritoff

"For every beast of the forest is mine, and the cattle upon a thousand hills. I know all the fowls of the mountains: and the wild beasts of the field are mine."

–Psalm 50:10-11

CONTENTS

To the memory of
Dorothy Chloe Cummings
my paternal grandmother
who influenced my life greatly as she modeled
reverence for God and all God's creatures

Introduction

Photos of furry creatures and social-media videos of cute animal antics ... books and movies of animal adventures ... these are popular because they evoke feelings of wonder, memories of beloved pets, joy and excitement of wildlife sightings, or perhaps sensory experiences of a trip to the farm. Here is what I believe about our relationship to animals:

- Animals are our fellow creatures, loved by the Creator.
- Animals can provide companionship, inspiration, and comfort.
- Animals can teach us about the Creator and how to relate to God.
- Animals provide metaphors of our lives that help us understand ourselves.
- Animals (especially those in the wild) represent elements of Mystery.

God cares for his earthly creatures. He created them, blessed them, called them "good." He saved the animals from the Flood and then made a covenant with "every living creature." Many Scriptures display God's care for animals. Old Testament laws protected animals. Jesus' parables affirmed and spotlighted them.

In *God's Creatures: A Biblical View of Animals*, Susan Bulanda asks: "Is it possible that God has put the desire to care for all animals in the hearts of many people ... God's love for his creation showing through humans?" Later she adds: "Could there be subtle lessons of love God gives us through our pets?"

I think you will recognize these reciprocal lessons of love—some subtle and some not so subtle—in the stories, poems, anecdotes, and reflections included in this volume.

Sometimes animals are mirrors for us to see ourselves more clearly. I have found my dog to be a barometer of my emotions. His responses tell me when I am getting anxious or when my words sound too harsh; he responds much differently when my tone of voice is sweet and cheerful. It makes me feel bad to see him put his ears back and watch me with a worried expression. It makes me feel good to see him wag his tail and smile at me.

Animals, both wild and domestic, also help us by calling forth our sense of awe. As Thomas Berry has said, we need all of creation, including the animals "to evoke a world of mystery, to evoke the sacred."

I continually wonder at the wilds of nature that can thrive alongside, often in spite of and struggling to adjust in the midst of, the civilized, tamed, domestic world. When a bird comes close and sings, when a deer steps out of the forest; these surprise sightings thrill. Finding myself sharing space with a wild creature, aware of each other, watching each other even for a moment, is a reminder of not only how different we are, but of what we have in common. Both the animal kind and my kind have breath. We communicate with body language and voice. We walk, run, choose mates, nurture families, search for food, seek shelter. And when we share moments of awareness and attention, the resulting experiential knowledge surely changes or affects us both in some way (hopefully not making us more fearful of each other), perhaps increasing our appreciation of our common creation.

We also share our lives with pets and, sometimes, farm animals. Our human friends learn to accept our animals as "part of the deal." In a deeper application, the slogan often seen on kitchen towels or plaques, "Love me, love my dog" could, I think, be re-phrased "Love God, love God's creatures." Theologians have said as much, and more.

The Celtic saint Columbanus exhorted, "Understand, if

you want to know the Creator, created things."

Orthodox scholar Maximus the Confessor taught the idea that creation (as well as Scripture) is God's book. "God is 'encoded' for us in everything he has made. We are surrounded on every side by his 'letters,' his 'analogies' in creatures...." Our part is to care for, as well as give attention and respect to, the creatures, and even to praise God on their behalf.

Protestant evangelical theologian (and bird watcher) John Stott wrote, "God has given to human beings a midway position between himself and the animals. ... In consequence, we combine the dependence on God that is common to all his creatures with a responsible dominion over the [animals] that is unique."

Catholic writer Charles Camosy adds, "Nearly all theologians now agree that the biblical dominion God has given human beings over creation is not a license to use and dominate, but rather a command to be caretakers and stewards."

I am thankful for all the dogs, cats, fish, chickens, ducks, birds, as well as the rabbits, squirrels, and deer that have been part of my life at different stages. I have cared for them, learned from them, and shared life with them. Many times when I or my family were facing challenging times, our hearts and spirits were lightened because the animals were there.

God, of course, is always there, everywhere, ever present to us; but God, who is spirit, does not have a corporeal body with skin, hands, and feet. Animals (as well as people) help God help us feel our loving, relational God's presence.

With all this in mind, I enjoyed compiling, editing, and writing a number of these sometimes-funny, often-touching, and always awe-inspiring experiences with animals. I hope our readers enjoy these stories, too, and find themselves giving thanks for God's creatures, the animals in our lives.

Catherine Lawton

Jeremiah (story on p. 40)

Weber (p. 48)

Bruna (p. 82)

Scout (p. 66)

OUR DOGS

"It's all about loving and being loved, I'd say."
–Shelly the dog

"The only people who can say that dogs do not have souls are those who do not know what a soul is or who have never been loved by a dog!"
–Fr. Richard Rohr

PAL
My First "Show" Dog

by Susan Bulanda

I was so painfully shy as a youngster that I was terrified if I had to stand up in front of the class at school to give a report. Yet here I was, on the stage of the junior high school with my dog Pal. We were about to perform in the ninth-grade talent show. *Was I out of my mind? What ever possessed me to agree to this?* I thought as I waited behind the curtain, ready to go on next. My knees were shaking and my heart was pumping so hard it hurt my chest. I cannot recall if it was hot behind the curtain or not, but I was starting to sweat.

We had practiced our routine flawlessly a number of times. Pal would jump through a hula-hoop covered with colorful paper, climb up and down a special ladder that my father had made, and lastly, he was to "sing" to the song, "How Much is That Doggie In the Window." I had taught Pal to bark when I raised my pinky finger and stop when I lowered it. I instructed the piano player to stop at each point in the song when the dog barked and then wait for Pal to bark two times. I stressed that the pianist was not to continue with the song until he heard two barks. My mistake! But I am getting ahead of myself.

The stage people set up my props, and then the curtain opened. I looked over the vast sea of faces; the whole school was there. Pal looked at me, and if I had not been so nervous, I would have paid attention to the twinkle in his eye.

The hoop was our first routine. I walked Pal (off leash) to the end of the stage as we had rehearsed, and told him to "stay." Then I walked to the other end of the stage and picked up the paper-covered hoop.

"OK, Pal," I called to him. "Through the hoop!"

Just as we had practiced, he ran across the stage right toward the hoop. But then, in a flash, he ducked under it.

I turned pink. I hoped the audience did not see the color of my face. What to do? I had not anticipated this. Taking a deep breath, I told Pal, "Go back and do it again."

He walked to the other end of the stage and stood there.

"OK, through the hoop!" I said in a sterner voice this time.

This time, Pal casually sauntered across the stage looking at the audience as he walked. When he got to the hoop, he stopped. Then he leaped through it!

The audience roared and clapped.

Whew, I thought. *One down and two to go.*

We walked over to the ladder. "Up the ladder," I told Pal.

He climbed up the ladder, paused at the top, stuck his chest out while he looked at the audience, then descended.

I relaxed a bit since that part of the act went smoothly. Now we had the song to do.

The piano was located below the stage, so everyone could see us on the stage. We walked over to the piano and I had Pal sit. The music started as Pal quietly sat there watching my face. And, I tell you, he had a grin on his face.

The music stopped. In perfect timing I raised my pinky and Pal barked two times then stopped when I lowered it.

The music continued and all went well until we got to the last part where Pal had to bark. I raised my pinky and Pal barked once. I stood there. Pal sat there, his tail gently swaying back and forth. The piano player was waiting. How violently can you raise a pinky? I couldn't stretch it any further. No bark. In desperation I looked at Pal and asked, "Where's the other bark?"

With that, he barked one more time.

The audience went wild. I found out later that they thought it was all part of the routine. Little did they know that it was only part of Pal's routine.

What a comedian!

SHELLY
Walking Through Empty Nest Syndrome

by Catherine Lawton

A muscular dog, a frisky cat, and a flock of chickens sharing a backyard aren't likely to comprise a peaceable kingdom on this earth. But that's how it turned out.

The day our son, David, left for college 600 miles away from home, my husband, Larry, and I began to feel the emptying of the nest. I cried. But we still had our teenaged daughter, Christina, with us. Two years later, though, when we returned to a quiet house after settling our daughter into the freshman women's dorm at the same university, empty-nest syndrome flared in earnest. I cried a lot. And without the buffer of children in the home, Larry and I were faced with getting to know each other again. Furthermore, without the daily interactions I had enjoyed with the kids, I felt rather afloat. I needed grounding.

Then came a puppy named Shelly. Only six-weeks old when I saw her at the local shelter, the sturdy, brown, bouncy puppy instantly won my heart. I couldn't resist adopting her. She had been labeled a Heeler mix. With her muscular build and slightly block head, most theories were that she was also part Pitbull or (as our Vet guessed) part Rottweiler. A mix for sure, that tiny puppy grew to be sixty pounds and quite attentive and protective.

For the next few weeks after adopting her, I carried baby

Shelly in my arms wherever I went. When I stopped by the church, when I shopped at the feed store, when I attended a board meeting of a local nonprofit, Shelly was with me.

Shelly came to our home during an El Niño year in Northern California. She adjusted quickly to sleeping in her crate beside our bed all night. My husband, bless his heart, would set his alarm, get up in the night, and take the puppy outside. Since it rained every day that year from early fall to late spring, he would stand out in the front yard with baby Shelly on a leash, holding an umbrella over them both until she accomplished her jobs. I appreciated Larry's willingness to do this (reminiscent of how he would get up in the night to fetch our crying baby girl and bring her to me to nurse eighteen years before).

The crate training and nightly routine worked. Shelly was house trained easily. Then I trained her to leash, which wasn't difficult (she loved walks), except that she was like a little bulldozer wanting to forge forward. First I walked her the four blocks to my sister's house. Those were lively visits because my sister had three dogs of her own. And our loyal dog who loved us so much, didn't instantly love everyone else she met—especially other dogs. Except there was one dog she adored—my sister's Rottweiler named Friedel. Probably Shelly had been taken from her mother too early. She needed a mommy and she chose Friedel as her maternal ideal.

The problem was, Friedel's lower canines had been removed, so she couldn't discipline Shelly with any kind of threat of a bite that would hurt. But, towering over Shelly, Friedel would snarl, teeth—sans canines—bared and lips curled back, while Shelly just kept cuddling up and kissing, kissing, licking, licking Friedel's snarling-but-longsuffering mouth. We laughed, then tried to console Friedel.

I was glad when Shelly was strong enough for longer

excursions on foot, because I love taking long walks through the neighborhood, along river paths, or on wooded trails. When I walk alone, I think and pray. When I walk with a friend, the activity lends itself to conversation.

Meanwhile, Larry would leave for work in the morning before we were wide awake enough for much conversation and return home in the evening and become engrossed in a home or yard maintenance project. He'd always been athletic—a basketball star in high school, college, church leagues, city leagues (and now in the National Senior Games)—but, except for occasional mountain hikes, he had never been one to just take walks. For him, an activity needed to be a game or have some purpose. Walk in the neighborhood?!

It took me some convincing to get him to try a walk one evening with Shelly and me. He somewhat skeptically set out down the street with us. But he brought along his basketball! And he dribbled it most of the way, stopping to shoot a basket whenever we passed a neighbor's portable backboard positioned near the street.

To say it mildly, that kind of walking was not conducive to conversation. "I was hoping we could talk," I said. He answered, "Talk about what?" But the next time we went out for a walk, he left his basketball home and, though walking didn't seem to provide him the same level of exercise it did me, we kept taking walks with our dog and gradually eased into a trekking camaraderie—observing nature around us, talking about our day, greeting people we passed, and basically getting to know each other again after the intense years of child rearing, church and community involvement, and career. Thank you, Shelly, for giving us a reason to get out and walk and talk together.

During those years we found other rewarding ways to fill the empty nest. Larry, still working full time, coached a boys' basketball team on the side. I founded Cladach Publishing during that time. We both worked with Laotian refugee kids in a Christian scouting program at our church.

But our evening walks with Shelly continued to keep our relationship freshly bonded.

And, gradually, we learned that the empty-nest years weren't always empty. They could be as elastic as a rubber band. The kids were usually home during summers, and they often brought friends home with them. These were memorable times, gathering on the back patio, eating homemade blackberry ice cream, playing ping pong, and philosophizing about life. Shelly was right in the middle of it all. She liked our children and their friends. Dogs seem to know when people are "our people."

A short time after both our son and daughter got married we had a delightful but unforeseen reprieve from the empty nest. Our son and daughter in law, who had been serving as volunteer missionaries in Europe, returned to the states needing a place to stay until they could get on their feet and make ends meet. They didn't have children yet, but they did have ... a cat! A small, round-faced and round-eyed black cat named Zorro.

I had not bargained for this. But what could I say?! They brought Zorro all the way from Montpellier, France. And he was cute! I—though not a "cat person"—had fond memories of a pet black cat of my childhood. That cat, Amos, had been not only a playmate, but a confidant. I would sit on the back porch with him, petting him and pouring out my problems to him. He would listen attentively and purr sympathetically.

Anyway, if you're a parent, you know how it is; we put up with a lot for our kids.

We settled on a household system that worked for all the people, things like taking turns cooking.... But could

Shelly and an active kitty cohabit the same house?

It worked out surprisingly. Cats, of course, have advantages that frustrate and bewilder dogs, and though Shelly was a smart dog, Zorro was a smart cat. And playful. And funny. And climbing the walls. It was okay until Zorro knocked a knickknack off the fireplace mantel. After that, he became an outdoor cat, at least during the day. Our daughter in law was hesitant at first, because we lived in an area with lots of trees, a creek nearby, and so various wild creatures sometimes visited our yard. However, Zorro thrived outdoors, often alarming us with his daring-do, but delighting himself in clambering over, under, around the large redwood beams above our patio, darting up fruit trees, and scrambling along fences. He kept an eye on Shelly and occasionally came near to commiserate briefly. Shelly was always aware of Zorro and seemed to actually like having a backyard companion, however frustratingly feline.

While our kids were growing up, our son, David, raised pigeons and our daughter, Christina, kept a flock of hens (and sold eggs). Now David decided he wanted to get a few pigeons again. At the feed store with David buying pigeons, I saw chicks for sale and thought, "Why not?" So I started a flock of hens again. This time they were my very own chickens. We still had the nice solid hen house Larry had built, as well as the pigeon lean-to. So our "back forty" came to life again.

I enjoyed my flock. Another corner of the empty nest was filling up.

When we first got the chicks, we kept them in a wire cage in the mudroom. Visitors would shake their heads at the sight: Zorro lounging on top of the cage gazing down at the peeping chicks, watching with interest (and appetite?). Shelly pressing her nose against the outside of the cage, seemingly licking her chops. But who can read the mind of a cat or a dog?—or a chicken, for that matter?

One chick was a runt, always a little different from the others. And she grew more slowly. While the others were greedily pecking their mash, that little chick would interact with Shelly through the wire cage. She liked to peck gently at Shelly's nose, perhaps getting some "delicious" tidbits and moisture. And Shelly let her. The dog seemed enamored. But people told us, "Just wait till you let those chickens loose. They're goners."

It didn't work out that way. Having watched and attended the chicks as they grew from babies to pullets, neither Shelly nor Zorro ever attacked a chicken. I have little doubt they might have chased and tried to "get" some random chicken outside our yard. But these were "ours" and part of our little family.

That little runt hen, though, even when full grown, took the brunt of Shelly's "friendship." They were always drawn to each other, and Shelly would show her dominance and ownership of her favorite hen by standing over her and licking her feathers, until the crouching hen was wet all over. When Shelly released it, it would shake and fluff out its feathers again with relief; but it never gave up on its devotion to that dog. I often intervened and got Shelly to leave the little hen alone so she could get back to scratching around for seeds and bugs with the rest of the flock.

After a few months, when our son and daughter-in-law were established in jobs and further schooling, they moved into their own apartment. We still saw them at church and various other times. And David stopped by most days to check on his pigeons and watch them fly in circles.

Speaking of circles, I had a path where I would walk around in the back forty. (A long hedge separated the immediate backyard with its lawn and rose bushes from the more unkempt part of the yard that contained hen house, pigeon lean-to, garden shed, a few fruit trees, garden plots, compost, and brush pile). While the chickens clucked, the pigeons cooed, Zorro darted about, up and down ... Shelly followed me, as I walked and sang praise songs, talked with God, released my concerns to him, and sought to listen to God's heart. When leaves fell in the fall, I loved the sound of their skittering and crunching underfoot. And when the green-encased nuts began falling off the spreading branches of the walnut tree, I discovered something.

The chickens liked walnuts! They would peck and peck open the green rind then the brown shell, and determinedly work out the nut meats. To speed up the process for them, one day I stamped on a walnut to crush it underfoot and the flock came running from all directions to peck out the nutmeat pieces. Shelly followed suit and found out she liked walnuts too. It became a game we played, a fun, bonding pastime for a few minutes a day as I stamped on walnuts and dog and chickens raced to the treats. Zorro was never far away. He would zero in on one hen, his bright eyes narrowed, his little ears erect, his body taught. Lion-like, he'd lower himself into a crouch and stalk, inching toward the chicken. Then he'd run for the pounce; but at the last second he'd veer sharply away and scamper up a tree. The chickens didn't pay much attention to his game, but Zorro seemed to derive wild satisfaction from it.

I called this my peaceable kingdom.

While our daughter-in-law was pregnant with our first grandchild, they moved away to the opposite coast of the U.S. David sold his pigeons back to the feedstore. But they left Zorro with us. So I still had my menagerie of dog, cat, and hens.

Then, in another year, after 25 years in that house where we raised our children, we ourselves were moving. We chose to move closer to one of our grown children, in this case our daughter and her husband and baby girl. We of course would take Shelly with us.

And the chickens? Well, when a prospective buyer saw plump hens scratching in the backyard, she was sold on the house! The young woman had always wanted to live in the country and have chickens, she said. It wasn't exactly the country, but a more affordable 50s-style ranch house in an unincorporated area with its own well and septic system, built on a one-half acre lot. A wonderful place for our son and daughter to grow up. So many memories! But they had grown, fledged, and left the nest. And, even with the animal companions, regular walks and trips together, church and community involvement, it wasn't the same. Besides, Larry said he was ready for a change, a semi-retirement from a corporate career and crowded commute.

And what about Zorro? We found no solution but to take him to the humane society. I didn't have the heart to leave him there myself. My brother-in-law, Curt, offered to do it for me. At the last minute before saying goodbye to that cute, fun little cat, I had an inspiration. I wrote out a page about Zorro, so the humane society people and any prospective adopters would have an appreciation for this special kitty. I hoped his unique bio would help preserve his life and convince a discerning person to give him a home.

During the transition as we moved into our Colorado house—making it a home, landscaping the yard, organizing our office, and getting to know our community—when Zorro came to mind I would feel a slight uneasiness, and probably even would breathe a prayer that Zorro would be adopted.

A few months passed. One day I received an email from a friend in California. She told me that while doing her morning workout, she was watching the local news channel. During a break in the news a woman from the animal shelter came on camera holding a small black cat. The woman's words caught my friend's attention: "This is Zorro. He is available for adoption. Zorro was born in France. He likes people, likes being outdoors, stays close to home, and is used to sharing space with a dog and backyard chickens. Wouldn't you like to adopt Zorro?" She was sharing the information from my letter.

As I read my friend's email, a smile of relief and joy broke over my face. Zorro was still alive! And, with such media attention, he would surely win someone's heart and find a home.

Meanwhile our dog, Shelly, adjusted quite well to Colorado and enjoyed exploring a new backyard visited by cottontail rabbits, squirrels, and an occasional fox. You can tell she continued to be my loyal, attentive companion by the following email I wrote on her behalf to our scattered-across-the-country family members:

Dear Family,

Life here is quieter since The Man started leaving early in the morning almost every day (to go to work again). I moped around at first. But I'm becoming pretty flexible, and now I just follow My Lady around all day and respond to whatever she says, such as: "Get up!" "Come back!" "Here's your breakfast." "Stay." "Where's your ball?" "Do you want a cookie?" "Let's feed the birds." "Don't bark, it's just Christina at the door." or "It's just the neighbors, or the mail, or FedEx." or "You stay here and watch the house. I'll be back pretty soon."

I spend a lot of time, like I am right now, lying under her desk by her feet (while she types out stories and emails), feeling secure, fulfilled, and happy. I have a purpose in life.

My Lady says she's proud of me for adjusting so well to being a "Colorado dog." It's not bad at all. Once in a while she takes me in the car when she goes to the drive-up window at the bank. I start licking my chops as soon as we drive into the bank parking lot. The teller always smiles and remembers to give me biscuits! Sometimes one big one, and sometimes several little ones, but they never last long. I love it!

Another nice thing about this Colorado life is that the vet comes to our house in his mobile unit and I don't have to get nervous going to those offices that smell scary and remind me of my past surgeries, and where strange dogs and cats lurk. This guy is gentle and he stands in the yard with us and he calls me a "sweetheart." He gave The Lady some stuff to help my ears and some candy that keeps away heart worms.

I still live for our daily excursions into the backyard. It's great to not have a fence, because they trust me to know the boundaries, and I'm an expert at that! I like to keep watch on the neighborhood. I know where other dogs belong and sometimes we bark "hello" to each other. Mornings, I like to sniff around to learn what wild visitors came in the night. And I like to chase my football. Or rub my tummy over the wood-chip mulch in the summer or snow in the winter. Or look for sticks. Or laze in the grass. Or stand close to The Man and My Lady in case they need my help when they're pulling weeds or tending the precious plants. My Lady sure is proud of her flowers! And she is almost as attentive to the wild birds as she is to me. Those little tweeters even come up close and look in the windows asking for more seeds whenever the feeders run out. Begging for more supper doesn't seem to work for me....

I sure can't complain, though. What a great life!

They also praise me for being so good with the new grandbaby, Caden. But it's old hat now. "Been there, done that." In fact, two-year-old Breanna is my good friend. We've reached an understanding (I finally got her trained to keep her hands away from my face and tail, and she plays fun games with me and gives me dog cookies).

I don't dwell on it (I'm a dog after all; I know My Lady and The Man think about you all a lot more than I do) but sometimes I'm reminded of the rest of the family. When My Lady came back from Connecticut two weeks ago, I sniffed and sniffed her suitcase and wagged my tail with joyous recognition of David and Hannah and little Isabelle and Matthew. And when a package came from Aunt Bev and Uncle Curt at Christmas time, or from the grandparents in Idaho, I got to enjoy more sniffs and tail wags.

I've got kisses and games and cuddles saved up for when I see you again. Meanwhile, I hope your Connecticut and California and Idaho lives are as good as our Colorado life.

It's all about loving and being loved, I'd say.
Yours faithfully,
Shelly

We had four grandchildren (and two more on the way) by the time our faithful Shelly died. We had entered a new era of life with more grace because Shelly walked with us through the years of empty-nest syndrome.

A DOG-NOSE MIRACLE

by Janyne McConnaughey

The door just barely opened and a long-nosed Sheltie peeked through the crack. My son, Eric, who was about ten years old, looked at the dog, then at me, and back at the dog before yelling, "Staff! It's Staff!"

About two months before, my friend and her husband had taken their dog up to their lake property deep in the countryside of Missouri. It was the Fourth of July weekend and Staff got spooked by fireworks and ran away. There were acres and acres of woodlands around the lake and the hope was he would find his way back. But he never did.

My son, who was just beginning to display his life-long devotion to dogs, had made friends with Staff and was devastated when he learned about his disappearance. He wanted to know what was being done to find him. I tried to console him with all the efforts the family was making, while at the same time, emphasizing how very impossible it might be to find him. The lake was in an isolated area and surrounded by miles and miles of wilderness. Wild animals, including predators, were abundant; but I tried to avoid mentioning that possibility!

Undaunted by Staff's improbable return, Eric began to pray every single night for the dog to come back home. Home was actually two hours from where he was lost, and the family was not always at the lake, so that added to the problem. Yet he had solid faith that God would hear his prayers. He never missed a night. He took seriously 1 Thessalonians 5:17, "Pray without Ceasing"!

"He prays for Staff every night," I told my friend.

"I am glad," she said and then commented on how God always seemed particularly attentive to the prayers of children. I both agreed and hoped it would be true in this instance.

I did wish Eric had chosen something much less like a miracle to test out his childlike faith. I wondered how it would affect him if the prayer was never answered; and Staff never returned. I tried my best to let him test out his faith without discouraging him; but I lacked even the faith of a mustard seed myself—until the phone call came.

"Staff is back!" my friend exclaimed.

I was stunned. It seemed completely beyond the possible. "How?"

Staff had ended up miles and miles away on a farm on the other side of a major highway. There were numerous fences between the lake and the farm and no direct roads. The family who owned the farm, where the starving dog arrived, nursed him back to health. They told the store owner in the small nearby town that they had found a lost dog that looked like a small Collie. My friend stopped by the store to pick up some items and mentioned about her lost Sheltie. The store owner made the connection. It had been two months and everyone had given up hope, except my son.

I was beyond excited and knew this was something that would live on inside this impressionable child who trusted beyond reason.

"Let me grab Eric," I told my friend. "I will be to your place in twenty minutes. When I knock, just let Staff peek out the door."

In the middle of his summertime ten-year-old activities, my son was less than ecstatic to be dragged off to my friend's house—especially since he thought Staff was no longer there.

He grumbled and complained, and I bribed him with a treat. We were on our way.

The plan worked perfectly. The look on Eric's face when Staff's nose peeked out of the crack was one I will always treasure.

I knew there would be prayers he would pray during his lifetime which would not turn out like this one. I understood there were so many factors involved—my friend continuing to ask if anyone had seen her dog, and the willingness of the farm family to care for the dog and search for the owner, and a small Sheltie's determination to keep looking for help. I wonder if he headed toward the highway to find his way to his home. So much went right, but so much could have gone wrong.

Eric, now in his thirties, has a profound optimism about life—even when things are going very badly. I often wonder if this experience provided a sense of hope at a developmental level which enables him to believe in the improbable and sometimes impossible. When the call came from my friend, I knew this as an opportunity to affirm his determination to believe God was listening to him.

As I write this, I long to pick up my phone and call Eric. I want to ask him if he even remembers. I wonder what his adult interpretation might be. But he is a church camp counselor this week. He struggled as a teen but eventually found his way to a life of ministry. Where he is today is probably the answer to any question I might ask.

Eric has been a youth pastor since college graduation and will begin teaching Bible this fall at a Christian high school. I am a firm believer in the experiences of childhood being the foundation upon which our life is built. I cannot help but believe that a small dog's nose peeking through a crack in the doorway was a divine intersection; one which will always look very much like a dog-nose miracle.

ROCKY II

by John Buzzard

When we were finally able to buy a house, my wife, Eva, and our two children clamored for a dog. Now that we were home owners, there was no excuse not to have one. During all our years of renting, a dog was always one of those things the lease prevented us from having.

"Please, Dad, can we get one?" my daughter Margie asked.

My son Jesse was always the quiet type, but I could see in his eyes that he hoped for my approval.

"All right. But you two are going to have to share in the responsibility of making sure he or she is fed and has plenty of water at all times."

"Yeah, yeah, we will!"

"And if the dog has an accident inside the house, that will have to be dealt with."

"Yeah, we know. That will be okay."

"And another thing. I'm choosing the breed. It has to be a German Shepherd."

The kids were okay with that; Eva not so much.

"I don't want a big, mean dog," she said.

"German Shepherds make great guard dogs and great pets. The dog will be completely loyal to you, but will defend you against any intruder who might break into the house."

Eva agreed.

The kids soon found an ad in the newspaper for German Shepherd puppies being sold on a farm about ten miles east of town. We went out there and got the last one. It was a male, which the kids named Rocky. Unfortunately, in less than a year, Rocky died of the parvovirus. Parvo was something we had never heard of. Through some research, I learned how contagious and lethal this virus is to dogs; especially puppies of the black-and-tan breeds. In any case, we were all devastated, and it was advised that we wait at least six months before getting another dog. This measure was supposed to ensure that the virus was completely gone from our property.

It had only been five months since the dog died, but Eva's birthday would be at the end of April, and I wanted to surprise her with a new puppy. I determined that, with the Lord's help, I was going to get another German Shepherd pup and make sure it had the parvo vaccination. The opportunity came when Eva and the kids left to run errands for a couple of hours. I drove to a house whose owners had placed an ad for German Shepherd puppies. I picked the most rambunctious male in the litter. Then I hurried home, gave the puppy a bath (he was covered with dirt), and then waited for my family's return. They were surprised to see me sitting in my recliner with a puppy on my lap.

"Whose dog is that?" asked Eva.

"Yours."

"What?!"

I repeated, "It's your dog. This is Rocky II. Happy birthday!" (Not until I said his name out loud did I notice it sounded like the movie title.)

Needless to say, Eva and the kids were overjoyed. There was a sudden frenzy of getting his bed and food and water bowls. Rocky proved to be an energetic fuzzball that immediately brought a lighthearted atmosphere to the house, something lacking since the first puppy had passed.

This poor little guy must have had three parvo shots in his first year. However, he didn't remain a little guy for long. The floppy ears became pointed and stood straight up, his squeaky yelps turned to deep barks, and bulky muscles covered his chest and shoulders. By the time he was two years old, he weighed as much as Eva. He scared off many pesky door-to-door salesmen, but one time when I drove him to a veterinarian appointment, he jumped onto Eva's lap and trembled with fear. Eva yelled at him, but I laughed.

There are too many humorous episodes involving Rocky II to recount. I once planted a sapling tree, only to have him dig it up and bring it to me as a stick to be thrown. There was the time I jumped into our swimming pool, but he thought I was falling in by accident, so he used his teeth to grab the back of my leg. I hollered in pain all the way to the bottom of the pool. When he was in the car with Eva, he knocked the gear-shifter into neutral while she was at a stop sign. She couldn't figure out why the car wasn't moving. And when Eva vacuumed the carpet in the house, Rocky would bark. He wanted to be vacuumed as well! He would lay his ears back, close his eyes, and act as if he was getting a massage while the suction removed the loose clumps of hair from his coat.

Since Eva is from the Philippines, naturally that's the type of food she cooks. Rocky was her biggest fan. Adobo, lumpia, lechon, pancit, fried rice, he ate it all. She would fill his bowl, and say, "That's my Filipino Shepherd."

Rocky had a bed in the living room, but he had another in my office, A.K.A. my man-cave. After the kids moved out, and Eva was away, he napped on that bed while I did my writing. As I typed out some manuscript on the computer, he would get my attention by using his long muzzle to poke me in the armpit. This meant it was time to have his ears scratched or his belly rubbed.

Eventually, he took on a new role as my unofficial service dog. Real service dogs are often given to veterans struggling with Post Traumatic Stress Syndrome. If nothing else, they provide much needed companionship. This was something Rocky was always willing to do. Several years ago, I was diagnosed with PTSD, not from my military service, but from being shot while working as an armored-car guard. There were the unexplained bouts of psoriasis, hives, and rashes that suddenly disappeared as quickly as they had arrived, only to reappear on another day and on another part of my body.

The short-term memory loss is bad, but the dark depression is the worst. At one point, I felt as if I could no longer handle the stress life was throwing at me. At work, I was suspended for a week pending an investigation to determine if I should be terminated. We had a new branch manager—a young administrator, still in his twenties, who felt all mistakes needed to be corrected by suspension or termination.

In my office, I worried about us losing the house and our savings. The story of David being pursued by King Saul in I Samuel 23 came to mind. "Lord, why is this happening to me? This matter is being blown way out of proportion."

God reminded me that he was working for good in this matter and I could trust him. Then I felt another poke in the armpit. Rocky stood next to me with a look of worry. I applied the usual treatment, by attending to the back of his ears and his belly. In a strange way, I felt better. The matter was in the Lord's hands. And I retained my job. A few months later, the eager-beaver manager was recalled to the corporate office in Dallas. Rumor had it, he was placed in a cubicle somewhere in the company's high-rise building and never bothered anyone else again.

Over time, Rocky's muzzle turned gray and his eyes began to cloud over from cataracts. He began to look frail and increasingly lost his footing. His hind legs were causing him problems. Then one day, he pooped in the house for no reason. No big deal, but it happened again and again.

Inevitably, the day came when it was time to make the phone call. I couldn't do it. Eva called the local humane society and made an appointment to have him euthanized. She made the appointment, but I was the one who had to take him to it.

It was a Thursday morning, and his appointment was at 11:00. Tucson is a vast city with only one humane society facility, so I would need about an hour to get there. The closer to 10:00 it got, the more upset I was becoming. I watched a rerun of *Hazel*, where the little boy found a stray dog that the whole family loved, but the dad was being a real hard-nose about it. I kept looking over at Rocky II, resting on his bed, completely unaware of what was about to happen.

When the show ended, I grabbed his leash and said, "Come on, Rocky, let's go."

Painfully, he stood while excitedly wagging his tail.

Tears immediately flowed down my face.

Because of Covid fears, I wasn't allowed in the building. A young assistant, with an ID dangling from the strap around her neck, and carrying a clipboard, came out and asked, "Hello, how may I help you?"

Whatever symptoms of PTSD Rocky had managed to take from me, came back in an instant. Here I was, a grown man crying behind my Covid mask with my Navy ball cap pulled down low. I could barely speak. Somehow, I managed to inform her I had an appointment.

"For Rocky?"

My voice cracked. "Yes."

I signed the paper giving them permission to euthanize my dog, and handed her my credit card. Rocky II pressed against my legs trembling.

When she returned to my car, she asked, "Do you want the leash and collar back?"

"No." I just wanted out of there.

The assistant took the leash, opened the door, and led Rocky inside the building. Rocky looked back at me to see if I was following.

Four hours later, Eva and I stood in the living room looking at the empty dog bed. Trying to keep her emotions in check, but failing, Eva blurted, "I miss my doggie."

"I know, I do too."

With hope in her voice, she asked, "Do you think it's true that all dogs go to Heaven?"

I put my arm around her. "I don't know if dogs are allowed in Heaven, but if they are, Rocky is more than qualified to be there."

It was a sad week, but we were both grateful to God that He allowed Rocky to be our dog for the past eleven years. No doubt, there will be other dogs, but for us, there will only be one Rocky II. And it is my hope that when I arrive in Heaven and sit to take it all in, I will feel that familiar poke in the armpit.

FINDING FREEDOM, EXPERIENCING JOY

by Gayle M. Irwin

A small wire cage confined him for nearly three years. The little Shih Tzu was just a number. No name. No affection. No lawn. No vet care. When the three-year-old male dog and his forty furry companions were removed from the puppy mill, little did they realize the joy their new-found freedom would bring, both to themselves and to others, including me.

Each dog received a name for the first time. The male Shih Tzu's moniker became "Stormy." For nearly a year, he lived at Hearts United for Animals, a rescue organization in southeastern Nebraska that liberates and rehabilitates canines from midwestern puppy mills. Staff and volunteers provide compassion and care, restoring these abused creatures to be adoptable companions.

Stormy's almond-colored eyes reached from the screen into my heart as I perused the Internet looking for a small canine companion. His round, furry face reminded me of an Ewok from the Star Wars movie series. I submitted an adoption application and after approval, my husband and I drove 600 miles one way to bring this little guy home. I had no clue how much this once-neglected pup would impact my life ... nor how much he needed a loving home to call his own.

The first few weeks weren't easy. We changed his name from "Stormy" to "Jeremiah." New home, new life, new name. The change took time for him, but with repetition he began responding to the name. His early years had lacked medical care, and while living at the rescue, a vet removed twenty-eight teeth from the little dog's mouth. Canines remained, including one that protruded, giving his jaw a unique look. Finding food he could eat that wouldn't upset his sensitive stomach proved daunting. So did leaving him alone.

My husband and I had prepared our home prior to our new dog's arrival, including the purchase of a doggie play-pen to house Jeremiah on the days we were gone for work. The wire enclosure provided standing and walking room plus a place for sleeping. On the first day we planned to be absent from the house, my husband and I spread pee pads inside the playpen and placed a cozy bed in one corner and water dish in another. We also provided two furry toys inside the area, forgetting Jeremiah didn't know much about such things. I returned home for lunch three hours after leaving our new dog in the pen. I discovered the enclosure had moved several feet from its original location, with Jeremiah whining and clawing at the wire. Instead of finding comfort in the small space, I realized he must have related it to the confinement he experienced at the puppy mill.

A few moments later, Jeremiah and our Springer Span-iel mix, Mary, spent time in the backyard. I observed them from the deck. A mellow, sweet seven-year-old, Mary was trained as a therapy dog. Jeremiah followed her around and seemed to imitate her actions. Then I realized Mary's ability to become our asset and Jeremiah's advocate. Before leaving for work again, I put up a baby gate to the kitchen which we used to keep charming Mary from becoming monster gar-bage hound. Doing so, and closing doors to the other rooms in the house, allowed Jeremiah to not be "caged" and to be near his new canine friend, thus giving him more freedom and the experience of joy.

Walks on a leash, which began as a struggle, became less of an issue the more we traveled the neighborhood. Jeremiah's original fear of the leather strap made me wonder if he'd experienced lashes from such an object. As weeks turned into months and daily walks became twice a day, I noticed a new lightness to his steps as if he recognized the accomplishment he'd made—a sense of happiness replaced the fear as we wandered the neighborhood and then stretched our journeys to other places, such as the pathway along the North Platte River, and trails near our mountain cabin. This puppy mill survivor, who had not known grass or sidewalks for the first three years of his life, began using his nose to sniff and explore. Squirrels and birds caught his attention as well; he was becoming a less fearful dog.

That confidence expanded. As I sat on the couch reading one evening, I heard a 'squeak.' I looked around the living room. My eye caught our recently adopted dog earnestly chewing on one of the soft, squeaky toys we'd purchased on our first trip to PetSmart with him. Jeremiah's nearly toothless mouth gnawed on the green, fleece-covered bone while his paws wrestled to hold the toy in place. Once he even clamped his jaws on the soft bone and shook it with vigor.

Tears formed in my eyes as I realized this was the first time since he'd come to live with us that he had engaged with a toy. The freedom to play, and the joy that gave him, broke forth like a geyser.

Not long thereafter, I again stood on our deck, observing Mary and Jeremiah in the backyard. The vast Wyoming sunshine bathed the greening yard with light, and though I needed to return to work, I basked in the warmth and hesitated to call the dogs inside. But I did. When Jeremiah heard his name, his head jerked up and his eyes looked my way. Suddenly, he sprinted across the yard, experiencing the freedom to run likely for the first time in his life. I grinned and cried simultaneously.

Psalm 126:5-6 came to mind. "Those who sow with tears will reap with songs of joy. Those who go out weeping, carrying seed to sow, will return with songs of joy ..."

Jeremiah started life as one sowing with tears: a small dog kept in a tiny cage, not known or being known, a number instead of a name. Now, he sailed across the yard in freedom, filled with joy, being known and loved.

I recognized those words of scripture also described me before coming to the Lord. When I realized the vast love of my heavenly Father, the immense sacrifice of Christ on my behalf, I found freedom and joy. I'm a daughter of the Most High King, and nothing can separate me from his love and mercy. 1 John 3:1 says, "See what great love the Father has lavished on us, that we should be called children of God! And that is what we are!" and in Romans 8:38, the Apostle Paul says, "And I am convinced that nothing can ever separate us from God's love. Neither death nor life, neither angels nor demons, neither our fears for today nor our worries about tomorrow—not even the powers of hell can separate us from God's love."

Such comforting words, such freeing and joyful reminders.

Jeremiah's travails caused harm emotionally and physically. Yet, his rescue and adoption brought freedom and joy. God's rescue, in the form of Jesus' death and resurrection and adoption into his family and the truth of his Word, bestows freedom and joy to those who trust in him. Each day I spend with my delightful Shih Tzu is a reminder of what an amazing gift is wrapped within the unconditional, sacrificial love given by my heavenly Father.

GRACE
The Distractive Therapist

by Beverly Coons

The abrupt death of my husband, Curt, thirteen years ago, left me with some huge challenges. My faith, family, and friends helped me enormously as I faced daily decisions and learned to walk a new way, to live a whole new life on my own. I had one other wonderful group of supporters that God gave me: my animals. Curt and I had three dogs at the time of his death. Linda Marr was the senior princess (and I was her servant); then there was intense, devoted Chocolette, the Chocolate Lab. Both of these older dogs died within the year of Curt's passing, adding to the big hole in my life. The third dog was much younger than her sisters, and very, very different. She proved capable of filling at least part of the hole.

Grace was a ninety pound Rottweiler with an attitude. You may wonder why I mention supportive pets and then write about Grace. Emotional support—or therapy, even—can take many forms. Grace was a "distractive therapist." She provided me with a whole new set of challenges that distracted me from all my other worries!

She was in many ways a liability as well as a comfort. She was devoted to me, but she was a dominant female, hardwired to be top dog in the canine pack, and very willing to punish all who crossed her. She was protective, as the poor unwitting man found out who ventured into my back yard to look at one of Curt's tools. I realized suddenly that I had sent him to the back, Gracie's realm. I raced back, just in time to save him. Grace had him pinned against the back fence. She made no noise but a low growl, baring her plentiful teeth and standing in her guard stance. I called to her, "Grace, it's okay! He's a friend!" Unconvinced, she held her ground until I came and stood beside the terrified man. Then she greeted him like an old friend. I think he decided he didn't want the tool, though.

Walking Grace was a daily adventure and required alertness on my account. No daydreaming, no getting lost in my problems on these walks. She was always on the watch for a dog that needed discipline. This meant we spent considerable time in neighbors' driveways with Grace on the "Sit" command and the pincher collar fairly taut, while she glowered at the dog walking by (do you have my permission to be here?), or the skateboard rolling by (all should die!). Over our six years alone together, I was remarkably successful protecting the world from my "protector," but there were a few fairly scary episodes.

The first happened the day her pincher collar broke. I decided to walk her without it, thinking she wouldn't notice just one time. As we rounded the corner at the end of my street, I spotted the neighborhood dog, Bailey, with his owner. Bailey liked to bark at Grace—and lunge. I could imagine he was calling her names and challenging her, while I held her tightly in a "Sit." Today, he and his owner were off the street, talking to a neighbor, and Bailey was quiet. I thought, "Okay, we can just scoot by and nothing will happen."

But Grace had spotted him as well. She played along until we were just opposite them. Then came the charge. She hunched her powerful shoulders and headed across the street towards Bailey.

I, of course, resisted, saying "No!" and yanking on the leash with all my might. But she was ahead, at the end of the four-foot leash. Slowly, inevitably, she dragged me across the street. I yelled at Bailey's owner, "Watch out! I can't stop her!"

The woman froze and stared as Grace continued her determined march to the poor pooch. Bailey, on the other hand, actually did something! He assumed a precautionary position by rolling over on his back and whining pitifully. When Grace reached him, she grabbed the nearest hind leg in her massive jaws, as I lunged for her collar and braced for the sound of crunching bones. But she just shook him! And let go.

She did not get a second chance. I twisted her collar and, with newfound strength, dragged her back across the street toward home. She went fairly willingly. After all, she had accomplished her task and was confused by my strong emotional response.

The next hour was filled with my weeping, a trip to the pet store for a new collar and treats to give Bailey. Then I hurried over to Bailey's home. I wasn't sure what my reception would be, but I had to go. When Stevie, Bailey's mom, opened the door, I burst into tears, apologized profusely, gave them homemade jam, dog treats and offered to pay any vet bills. Stevie hugged me, smiled, and assured me Bailey was fine—no broken bones, no broken skin, nothing. *Phew!*

Our walking route changed after the Bailey event, and peace returned. But Grace wasn't through with my "distraction therapy" yet. It was a gorgeous evening, almost sunset with piles of clouds in the west, providing a canvas for a spectacle of light and color. I paused to take in the moment. Grace waited beside me; all was quiet.

While I reveled in the sunset, she was watching for other things. Around the corner behind us came an enemy, one she had longed to confront, to stop, to show who was boss! She waited in silence while IT glided down the middle of the empty street. The teenaged rider of the skateboard was blissfully unaware. Suddenly, my peace and the skateboarder's evaporated as Gracie took action. With a deep roar she tore the leash from my hand and lunged into the street after her prey. I turned just in time to cry a warning to the unsuspecting kid. Not in time. She grabbed the skateboard from behind, giving it a mighty shake and tossing it away. The boy was, by then, lying in the street, ignored by the triumphant Grace. Happy with her success, she returned to me. I was halfway to the boy, voicing my concern for him. He jumped up, chased down his skateboard and left as quickly as he could. At least I knew he was okay.

Life with Grace was not all wild and terrifying events. She was devoted to me, followed me around the house, and understood almost everything I said. Once I saw a mole moving just under the surface of the garden soil. I said, "Grace, get the buggy!" and pointed. She immediately thrust her big nose into the soft earth and snatched the poor mole, presenting its now-still little body to me. Now that's devotion!

WHAT'S IN A NAME?

by Janyne McConnaughey

His name on the day we adopted him was PB&J (Peanut Butter & Jelly). I said, "Really?" We lived in our RV at the time. I could not imagine myself at the RV dog park yelling, "Peanut Butter & Jelly, time to go!" We had to think of another name. He didn't really seem to respond to that name, anyway. Did a worker just name the stray dog while eating her lunch?

Taking Weber for a walk is risky. He is a small dog who has illusions of his prowess. For instance, my Long-haired Dachshund mix is convinced he is up for the task of taking on the K-9 Unit German Shepherd who walks by our house. No, Weber, that is a bad idea. Thankfully that powerful force of nature is well-trained. Not so with other dogs.

During Weber's short life, my husband, Scott, and I have rescued this small dog three times. One time a cat attacked him; it is inexplicable. He doesn't bark at every dog; there must be characteristics he considers dangerous. I have explained to him, "Weber, taking on big dogs is not your purpose in life." He ignores me. After a dog bit me during a rescue attempt, and then Weber was attacked two more times, I no longer feel comfortable walking Weber alone. This is disappointing.

Most of the time, Weber is exactly who we needed when we adopted him. He was a stray from New Mexico (like me). We fell hopelessly in love with him at first sight, but he tricked us. "I do not want a dog who sheds," I said adamantly. He didn't—not one single hair on my black pants when he greeted us before the adoption. Ever since then, I have been drowning in his fur. Then I said, "No dog can be on the bed." He sleeps there now—in his own bed of course. Most importantly, he has curled up beside me while I wrote three books in three years. All is forgiven.

We really had no good reason to adopt a dog. We were having more fun going to look at dogs and cats than actually considering adopting one. We are really cat people. One time we had six cats. How that happened is a very long story, but not Weber's story. Oddly, Weber has many cat characteristics, but we didn't have to figure out where to put a litterbox in the RV. I said no to that idea.

And then we saw Weber.

He had a cone on his head, and all we could see was his beautiful reddish fur and curly tail. The two crazed adults trying to get his attention could not distract him from workers on the other side. So, we went to the other side and nearly had to lie on the floor to see him. That was when it happened; we fell in love with a dog.

But his name had to change.

Why did two adults living in an RV choose to adopt a dog? Because dogs and RVs just go together? Uh, no; that wasn't why. It was our therapist who suggested a dog would be good for us. I would eventually learn that therapy and dogs often do go together. Weber became our own personal therapy dog. So we named him Weber—because our therapist's office was located on Weber Street.

Weber thrived in the RV park, where Scott eventually became manager. He tried to chase the squirrels, knew the employees, and tried to jump into any golf cart that drove by. His favorite activity was to sit proudly beside Scott and tour the RV park as if he owned it. In the evening, we would sit together outside the RV and greet people who passed by. He considered everyone a friend. And he was great about all the dogs who shared the dog park with him—until the day one attacked him. That was when the dog bit me (thankfully, it was winter, and I had plenty of layers on!). Now sweet, small Weber believes his job is to defend me.

He may need to defend me, but Scott is his person. He senses when it is time for him to come home and has disrupted many a Zoom meeting. If we take him in the car, I can go inside, and Weber calmly waits for me to return. If Scott goes inside, he whines until he returns. Scott is his person; I am his responsibility to defend.

When Weber was a year old, we moved. There was a lot of chaos involved in that, but while Weber was with us, he was fine. It was March. We needed to drive from Colorado to Washington while dodging winter storms across Wyoming, Utah, Idaho, and Oregon. Weber never rode in the car for more than ten minutes before we began our eight-hour treks. And he always got sick. So, armed with anti-nausea medication, we started out on the trip with trepidation.

The veterinarian's famous last words were, "He will probably sleep the whole way." No, Weber never slept. He sat between us, mesmerized by the moving landscape as if standing guard with our guardian angels as we traveled. We took one more trip with him; it was the same. Weber never relaxes in a car. He is always happy when we pull up to a drive-through. The dog was born to travel.

We would be living with our daughter and family. So the next complication was integrating Weber into the household with our daughter's dog. The advice from the owner at her kennel was to take Weber to doggy daycare and let the two dogs meet on neutral ground. They played together for two days, and when we picked them up, they both looked surprised to get in the car together. They have coexisted peacefully for two years now. Understanding now that Weber believes he is my protector, this was the best advice!

Weber still gets concerned if we appear to be packing. He loves my daughter and grandchildren but does not like for us to be gone. He loves the life he inherited. Our current challenge is our newest addition, a black kitten who doesn't like the fact that Weber can jump up on the couch where he thought he was safe. In time we will all settle in.

Weber is a dog of patterns. Having so many people in the house during the Covid-19 pandemic often disturbed his routines, but he was never disappointed when grandchildren appeared.

In the evenings, Weber wants us to both be sitting in the bed watching a show, reading, or scrolling on our phones. As night approaches, it is not OK for Scott to sit in a chair, though. Weber is a creature of habit and endearingly wants his humans together.

As I think about the past few years, so much has changed, and we have faced so many challenges and adjustments. Yet, Weber has remained steady, protective, adventuresome, and comforting. He has been the calm in the middle of our storms—as any good therapy dog should be. We wish that the traumatic day in the dog park had not happened, but we understand trauma; and he is perfect for us in every way. Weber, the therapy dog, was aptly named.

BOGAR
A Dog In the Holocaust

by Kathy Rubin
as told to Susan Bulanda

One special day in 1939 Papa came home from work and called to us, "Children, children! Come see what Papa brought home!" We all ran to him, excited. On occasion, Papa would bring home a special treat for us, such as our favorite bread or a cheese round and sometimes sweets.

As we ran to see what Papa had brought, we did not see a package in his hand. But he was smiling his biggest smile, so we knew that he must have something. Then his coat wiggled and from under it a little black nose appeared.

"Papa, Papa, what is it?" We all asked, my big sister jumping up and down and clapping her hands. We couldn't wait; we grabbed at my father's coat to get it open. Nestled against his warmth was a small, furry puppy. Papa took the little ball of black fluff from his coat and handed it to us. We all wanted to pet and hold it. We sat on the floor and took turns cuddling the puppy.

His eyes were like liquid chocolate and he gave us little kisses as he wiggled from one person to another. Mama had come into the room to see what all of the excitement was. She did not say much, but I saw her glance at our father with the look that said, "What have you done?"

Mama sighed as Papa shrugged his shoulders and

gave her a look that said, "I couldn't help it."

We named the puppy Bogar, and it did not take long for all five of us—my parents, older brother, sister, and me—to fall in love with him. We loved to hold him and bury our faces in his soft, shiny fur. Bogar even won Mama's affection. After all, how could you resist such a bundle of love?

Bogar did many funny things that made us laugh. One time he decided that Papa's pants made a good toy and grabbed onto them as he tried to walk out the door. We all laughed so hard, we could not get Bogar to stop. After that we all tried to get Bogar to grab our father's pants legs when he walked through the room. Bogar, however, was smarter than we were; he knew Papa did not find this pastime amusing.

Another time when we were all outside playing, Bogar saw a butterfly and started to chase it. The butterfly flew in circles and Bogar tripped over his own feet chasing it round and round. We rolled on the ground laughing, then imitated him by twisting our legs and falling over.

Bogar had a keen sense of smell. If we were outside, he would alert us as soon as Mama started to cook or bake a special treat. His favorite meal was dinner, since he always got a scrap of meat or other leftovers.

Although there was an undercurrent of tension in our community in Hajdúhadház (a town in the Hajdú-Bihar county, in the Northern Great Plain region of Hungary) due to the anti-Semitic feelings and the war that had started, Bogar brought us happiness and joy. When we played with him, we entered a trouble-free world of love and joy. It was comforting to snuggle with Bogar. Often all of us kids would lie prone in the shade of a big tree, on the grass in the summer with Bogar next to us and make up stories or share a story from one of our books. These were some of the best times.

Bogar never grew big; he weighed only twenty pounds. He was all black and of undetermined heritage. He seemed to sense our trials and would rest his little head on an arm or leg, or curl up in a lap, sometimes sleeping or just gazing into our eyes. All of us would wonder what he was thinking, and what did he feel?

He made us laugh and was a constant source of joy, amusement and companionship. Sometimes Mama sat in her favorite chair to read a book, and Bogar would jump up into her lap and fall asleep. He especially liked to do this when the weather was cold or wet outside.

I, especially, bonded with Bogar. He followed me everywhere. Many times he and I would sit together alone and I would tell him all of my secrets.

I remember one time when we heard bombs in the distance. Our parents were frightened and could not hide their fear from us. That night I hid Bogar in my bed, under the covers with me. Somehow, he made me less afraid. We kids would hear stories about the war. And even though our parents and other grown-ups would not talk about it in front of us or within our hearing, they could not hide from us the worried looks and tense whispers that passed between them.

My friends and I would have our secret meetings and share the rumors we heard through the children's grapevine, as well as bits of conversations that we overheard. Those of us who had dogs would include them in our secret meetings. Somehow their presence made us feel safer.

Our family managed to survive the first five years of the war because Hungary did not enter the war until March, 1944. However, the war affected us all; for example, my father was taken several times into Forced Labor in the Hungarian Military starting in 1943.

Even Bogar hated the sound of planes and shooting.

Before we could hear it, Bogar would growl and raise the hair on his back when an airplane flew near.

Then the unthinkable happened, the thing we all feared. In June of 1944, we heard a commotion outside. Through a loud speaker the soldiers told all Jews to line up in the street. My parents had told us that this might happen and not to be afraid.

We had no place to run to or to hide. The soldiers came into the houses and told everyone to get ready to leave. We were only allowed to take one suitcase each. We rushed to grab some clothes and a few other things as the soldiers waved their rifles threateningly at us. We heard shots fired in the distance.

I saw my friends—our neighbors, the butcher, the doctor, and the banker—all of the people I grew up knowing and loving. They were standing, cowering and crying in the street. There were young people, middle-aged people, and the elderly trying to stand on feeble legs with help from their relatives.

As soon as we were lined up in the street, we were marched to the ghetto. We had no warning and no time to make provisions for ourselves or Bogar. We only had time to leave Bogar free outside. I prayed to God that he would be safe. But to my horror, when I looked around, I saw that Bogar was following us to the ghetto!

"Go home!" I cried. "Go home, Bogar." But he did not.

Dogs were not allowed in the ghetto, so as we passed through the gates, the soldiers chased Bogar, trying to hit him. I tried to run back to him, but my father held me by the arm and forced me to stay. I had never felt so helpless.

I thought I heard Bogar yelp, but I could not be sure, since I could not see him, and we had no idea where he was or what was happening to him. Though afraid and uncertain about our own fate, we also worried about Bogar. Who would take care of him? How would he survive?

For three weeks we were kept in the ghetto in Hajdúhadház. After three weeks we were again lined up in the street.
We were herded out of the ghetto and forced to walk to the
train station.

I looked around as I left the ghetto. I am not sure
whether I wanted to see Bogar or was hoping that he would
be gone. But I couldn't stop from looking. And as we left the
ghetto, to our surprise, Bogar was right there beside us. My
dear, sweet Bogar had waited outside of the ghetto for us.

Initially I was thrilled to see that he was alive, but when
he followed us all the way to the train station, my heart
sank. I couldn't keep tears from running down my face. I
anguished over what Bogar would do. Would he follow the
train? Would he be killed under the wheels of the train?
Would someone shoot him? Poor Bogar did not know we
would have to leave him again. What would happen to our
precious dog? All I could think of was Bogar, not even
about myself. Maybe by thinking of Bogar I was able to
handle my deeper fears. We had all heard stories about the
camps.

Our family survived the next year in Grafenegg, Aus-
tria, where I worked in forced labor doing farm work. After
that we were sent to Theresienstadt in Czecholslovakia. We
had little to eat and lived in horrible conditions. During
the first few weeks we would complain to our parents that
we were hungry. But we quickly realized everyone was
hungry and there was nothing we could do about it. We
did guard our meager possessions and food carefully. We
stayed together for protection because other people would
steal our food or clothes if we were not careful. Life in the
camp was a constant fight for survival.

We were never personally threatened. But we heard
rumors that caused us to wonder from day to day whether

we would be shot or tortured. And we all prayed for Bogar. It helped me to think of him instead of myself. I would curl up under my coat and pretend he was there for me to hold and tell secrets to. In my mind I would relive the fun times we used to have together. Thoughts of Bogar gave me hope.

Then on May 5, 1945 we were herded to the middle of the camp. This was not unusual, since the guards would check to see that no one had escaped, and to remove the bodies of those who had died in the night. But this time a murmur, an excitement moved through the line. I did not understand and was too weak to care very much anymore. If it had not been for the hope of seeing Bogar again, I would rather have given up and died. At least I would not be hungry or cold anymore. But I had promised Bogar that I would come back for him.

This time, on that glorious day in May, 1945, we were free! We were herded up and sent out to fend for ourselves, but we were free. We were alive and all of my family had survived. We started the long walk back to our home. It was the only place we could go.

I'll never forget walking that final mile. Because we were all so weak, we did not talk. But in our hearts, we wondered if Bogar would be there for us. I saw my parents and sister and brother look around as we got closer. I strained my eyes to see if I could spot Bogar. How I wished he would be there for us. How I missed him and wanted to hold him, tell him all that had happened, tell him that I really had not wanted to leave him, and that we were sorry. I wanted to cry into his soft, comforting fur.

We drew closer and closer to home, but no Bogar. No happy bark, no wiggling puppy, no soft fur. When we reached our house, we settled into what was left of our home. People had ransacked it looking for food, stealing anything they wanted. But at least we had a roof over our head, a stove to cook on and beds to sleep in. Some of our clothes were left, and some of our household goods. We needed everything that was left in order to survive. We established a routine of looking for food and fuel, and putting our lives back together.

"Papa," my sister, brother and I asked, "do you think Bogar will come home?"

"Dear children," he replied, "we will pray for him and keep hoping, but I want you all to be happy that *we* are all here. God will take care of Bogar."

We still longed for Bogar. Our home didn't feel the same without him.

Every day I would walk around our community, hoping to see Bogar, praying that God would bring him home to me and my family. I asked everyone I met if they had seen him, but most people were not sure; they did not remember what he looked like. They were busy trying to survive and did not pay much attention to stray dogs. Many dogs roamed the area. Some people I asked thought Bogar was dead, others thought they saw him run away. This was understandable, since they may have seen him follow us to the ghetto and thought he was gone.

The days passed and I could not find him. I was not strong enough to walk far or I would have walked back to the ghetto and train station to look for him. Slowly my hopes diminished. We were all thankful that we made it through the war and that we were still alive. We were joyful to be reunited with some of our neighbors and friends and to be able to worship at the synagogue again. But we mourned the loss of one family member: Bogar.

We had heard stories of dogs being caught and eaten, or being beaten or shot by soldiers. The bigger dogs would attack the smaller dogs as they starved to death. It wrenched my heart to hear these stories.

I kept thinking that Bogar hated the sounds of war and the soldiers so much that he would try to escape. But how could he find food? I knew that, to survive, people had caught and eaten all the animals they could get. I wondered, *What will be left for Bogar?* Then I remembered that he was small and he would not need much food to live.

A month later, I was walking down the road about a mile from home, still hoping to find Bogar when I saw a dog that looked like Bogar. I thought my eyes were playing tricks on me. My heart skipped a beat and I held my breath. I was so afraid to call his name because it would hurt so much if it wasn't him. Hesitantly, I called out, "Bogar! Bogar!"

The dog stopped and looked, frozen in place. Then like a shooting star, he ran to me, jumping and licking my hands and face. It was Bogar, my sweet, wonderful Bogar!

I knelt down and hugged him for a long time. I felt so happy and relieved. I thanked God for taking care of him. For the first time since we were taken away, I felt peace and hope. God did care.

The two of us hurried home as fast as our weak bodies could, and I burst through the door shouting to the family, "Bogar's home!"

We all hugged and kissed him, then we all hugged each other, tears in everyone's eyes. Next we gave him some of our precious little food, water, and a soft, warm place to sleep. After we got over our excitement, we saw that Bogar had had a rough life while we were gone. He was thin, his coat did not shine, and there was a haunted look in his eyes.

The next day I again asked people if they had seen

Bogar in the past year. When some people saw him, they remembered. We found out from people in our neighborhood that he had lived on the street, stealing food when he could.

For the next year we had our wonderful Bogar with us. Then when he was a little over seven years of age, he got sick and died. It meant a lot to us that for one glorious year our family was complete. When Bogar died, we all mourned deeply.

AISHA

by *Alice Scott-Ferguson*

She may have been but a scant six or seven pounds—so little and light—but large and beloved beyond measure was our Maltese named Aisha, a name borrowed from a place name in my homeland. We always seemed to have a sheep dog named Aisha in the Scottish Islands of my childhood, so the tie was strongly sentimental.

I chose her name. But she chose me. We bonded through the many light-filled days of laughter and travel and living near extended family in several states. Then, as companions traveling through a tunnel of bereavement, we entered the darkness, clinging and grieving together over her limited loss of limbs and of one gone who loved us both so well.

A birthday gift from my Colorado family, she was delivered at eight weeks to the appointed place by her breeder. All the excited new owners were gathered in a Denver hotel room where the floor was littered with newspapers. Lots of little white puffs of dog danced around the room. The puppies had already been designated to their respective owners; but my husband and I did not know which one of those delights was ours.

It was there I first felt those faithful little paws on my legs, the first of a million times during her fourteen-year tenure on planet earth. I still recall that touch, barely discernable, light as a floating feather. I looked down into that tiny face, those bright, love-filled eyes locked onto mine, and we knew we belonged together. The breeder then confirmed that this particular puppy had already been assigned to me. And Aisha already knew: She chose me!

Soon I was saying daily, "Let's go into the car; let's go walkies, Aisha girl!"

She sat still but for the brief time it took to click the leash into her pink, shiny stone-studded collar. Our mile walk around the park was sheer joy for us both. As we regularly did the circuit twice, she never flagged, her tiny steps a million miles a minute on the olfactory offensive, as always. My gaze, on the other hand, looked skyward scanning the changing of the seasons as told in the trees, which were planted primarily in groups of threes. Years later I memorialized them in a poem I entitled "Three Trees, Three Years," for it would take that long before I could ever walk there again after she no longer trotted beside me in her pink collar or, in the winter, sporting her cozy plaid coat.

THREE

Three trees
their bare lacy branches
silhouetted against cerulean sky
Three years
since I walked this park
with my forever-missed doggies
Today I breach the pain
and take a solo stride
Such was the grip of grief
Three trees
Three years

Only one other solicitation elicited louder barking than going for a walk. "Ready to see the gBoys?"

Ethan, the youngest grandson, was often her dog sitter in our absence. They were deeply devoted to each other; so much so that on leaving him, she birthed an agonizing cry of grief from a low register of despair that we heard on no other occasion. Another unique vocalization, in higher, happy pitch was reserved only, but always, and at the exact same turn on the road, when she announced the approach to our daughter's house where another Maltese puppy lived!

Her enthusiasm for life and love was endless. Her sense of fun and play were especially precious when engaging with our big, gentle Chesapeake Bay retriever, Bruna.

Bruna would bend down to roughhouse her and Aisha would tantalize Bruna with swift, out of reach moves. They were our duo of dear dogs for most of her life, traveling with us to our holiday beach home in Florida where Bruna, web-footed and fitted for the water, swam without stopping, while Aisha, not so equipped, followed her and momentarily disappeared in a tide pool! The life force is strong! In seconds (which seemed like agonizing minutes), she came shooting upwards to the surface by some primitive survival mechanism!

Safer and more secure was her favorite place; on my lap. Nowhere was this truer than on our motor home journey of over 3,000 miles from Colorado to Alaska and back; her wondrous warmth permeated my skin in the chill of the cold climes, and my human heat hovered over her tiny frame.

If Aisha wasn't on my lap, she was in the crook of my husband's arm. People referred to her as "his purse" for she was a forever visitor to family gatherings. His love for her was fierce, tender, and true.

On the night of his stroke, he did what he always did—the last duty of the day—Jimbo, as the doggies knew him, put Aisha to bed. The ensuing days dragged into long months of rehab and then into the aching, weeping world of home hospice care, where she was with my husband, Jim, constantly—cuddled up close, consuming his warmth, sharing his privation and pain. He, fumbling for her with frail hands, groped to stay grounded to the earth now slowly slipping from his grip. She was there till the end. The little dog of boundless energy had already suffered two spinal column strokes of her own and now knew her own limitations of movement in time and space. I have no doubt they both experienced one another in their brokenness just as acutely as they did in their wholeness and wonder of life-giving love.

The day of my devoted dog's departure was not when she almost drowned in a Florida coastal tide pool.... Nor was it due to her debilitating strokes from which she so courageously rallied and continued to run even with scissor-locked hind legs!... But neither was it the day she snuck out, past the no-longer-attentive Jim, who was working in an open-door garage, and headed out to sniff the pavement across a busy street. She was miraculously seen, and rescued, by none other than a loving Maltese owner!...

No! It happened in the cold, merciless morning of another kind of "knowing." It was time to make that most agonizing of all decisions, to let her go. I had to direct the veterinarian to stop a beating heart. He remarked, "She waited as long as she could so you would not be alone!" So fourteen months after my husband died, she, too, took flight.

If it is true, as science definitively declares, that energy cannot be destroyed, then the particle form that comprised my beloved Aisha, the essence that was housed in that container of soft, silky sweetness, those love-filled black eyes, and that damp, nuzzling nose is still out there. Somewhere! In the long grasses where her ashes are scattered in the meadows of Montana she so loved to explore? Resting with the remains of the one who carried her in the crook of his arm? Scenting the perfume of paths through sparkling stars? Snuggling on the Savior's lap?

She lives on forever.

"It's OK, baby girl, see you again…soon. I love you!"

SCOUT
My Soul Mate

by Susan Bulanda

I was involved in K9 Search and Rescue and I wanted a special dog. I had a friend who knew Beaucerons. She went to France every year to visit her parents, so I had her pick out a Beauceron puppy for me to use in search and rescue (SAR) work. This dog, who I named Scout, was to become my soul mate.

THE BABY

When Scout was one year old my husband and I were blessed with being able to adopt a beautiful baby boy from Korea. I will never forget the night we brought Tom home. Ness, my husband's Border Collie who did not particularly like children, took one look at the baby, gave a canine "hur-rumph," and walked away with the attitude, "Don't expect me to like him."

Scout on the other hand, took one look at Tom and, if I had to put words to his reaction, it would be, "Oh, for me?! Thank you." Scout was Tom's guardian and protector from then on. No matter what or where we were, he was always there watching. If we were by a body of water, Scout was between the water and Tom. If Tom was sleeping on his blanket on the floor, Scout was right beside him. When Tom learned to walk, he did so while holding onto Scout's collar.

Scout became the first Beauceron to do SAR (search and rescue) work in the United States.

THE TORNADO

The phone rang at two a.m. My husband woke me up with, "We have a search." The adrenalin kicked in and I jumped out of bed. My uniform shirt was in the washing machine, still wet because I had not put the load in the dryer. I grabbed a pink t-shirt and put on the rest of my gear. The dogs, who always knew when it was time to go to work, were dancing around our feet. We woke our son, got him dressed, and within fifteen minutes had our gear packed and were on our way to a nearby town.

A housing development had been hit by a tornado. One family had been killed. The full force of the tornado had directly hit their house and only the basement remained. Another family was missing. Our job was to search the wreckage, looking for the missing family.

It was balmy out, but we could smell the scent of destruction. The fumes from rescue vehicles, the smell of fuel, the scent from the food wagon. We could hear the hum of people talking in person and over the radios.

The staging area for rescue personnel was buzzing, and the staging area for the residents of the housing development was busy, as rescue personnel made assessments.

After a briefing, I headed with the structural team to the destroyed houses. Scout calmly walked by my side. Our mission was to search through the remains of the houses to look for the missing family.

The K9 police officer on the scene said to me, "Sue, don't do it; you'll get hurt."

"We train for this, Paul. Don't worry."

I headed for the first house we were to search.

"OK, Scout," I said. "Let's clear the area."

I gave Scout his disaster command.

We climbed up the pile of debris that had been a house, then we crawled down into the basement, looking for the missing family. We did this for every house that had been destroyed.

Time after time Scout gave me the "all clear" signal, indicating that there were no bodies, dead or alive in the debris.

Finally, we cleared the development. The family was not there. A few hours later, it was determined that they were away on vacation.

Tired and dirty, we headed home, mission accomplished.

MISSING DIVERS

It was a raw weekend in the winter when we got the call. Two ice divers were missing. They were last seen diving in a deep quarry.

One side of the quarry was a sheer rock cliff and the other side was accessible. I pulled on extra warm clothing and then put Scout's search vest on him. We were assigned a diver to go on the ice with us. On the far end of the quarry was a waterfall where the water had not frozen. Scout and I had to search that area since scent might rise at the edge of the ice. For safety reasons I put a harness on Scout with a long-line going to me. I, in turn, had a harness on with a long-line going to the diver who was suited for cold water. Thus we were prepared. If Scout fell in, then I could pull him out. If I fell in, the diver could pull me—or both me and Scout—out of the water.

We stepped onto the ice. Even though it was cold, there was a fog hanging over the quarry. This made it feel even colder. I gave Scout the command to search, and he led me across the ice. We both walked carefully, searching drill holes that the divers had cut in various locations to allow scent to rise. We moved on, he sure-footed, me slipping ever so slightly with every other step. I was nervous; we had to walk as close to the unfrozen water as we could. I trusted Scout, though; he would alert me to any dangers such as the ice cracking.

At one point Scout gave me a signal that he had located scent. To verify it, my husband brought his dog, Ness, out and let him search. Ness gave the same signal in the same area. The bodies were found nearby, about sixty feet down.

Scout and I worked together for almost eleven years. He became my soul mate. Of all the animals I have owned, none can compare with Scout. He was courageous and bold, but always gentle with people.

BUSTER
The Problem PK

by Catherine Lawton and Beverly Coons

As PKs (preacher's kids) in the days when ministers moved more often than they generally do today, we faced adjustments of a new town, new school, new church, new neighborhood every few years. Our pets provided us a source of constancy, entertainment, and companionship.

When we girls were ten and eleven, we got a free puppy somewhere—tiny, brindle brown, with big ears. He was half Boston Terrier and half Toy Pinscher. Mom said he looked like Buster Brown (of the shoe brand), and the name fit perfectly. We proudly took our puppy to the neighbor lady to show him off. She stepped out the kitchen door in her apron and greeted us with a smile. Then she declared, "That puppy is so ugly, he's cute!" Our feelings were hurt by the first part of her sentence, but the second part helped make up for it.

We told Mom what Mrs. Hart said. "Well, she's probably right. But we don't care. We love him!" And we did.

As PKs, we were expected to perform when asked (or told to), to speak politely when spoken to, be good examples to other kids, and otherwise be quiet, well-groomed, and unobtrusive. With a few glitches, overall we fulfilled those expectations. Buster, on the other hand, as part of our parsonage family, proved to be a bit of a problem PK. He was known to delay or disrupt church services, wasn't always friendly (even once biting a church leader), was known in the community as a bit wild, took too many risks, didn't value cleanliness and neatness, and sometimes forgot to show reverence.

It would take a whole book to tell you all the Buster stories. He wasn't a cat, but he did live about nine lives considering how he somehow survived one memorable event after another.

Buster was a little dog with a big attitude. A true family pet, he belonged to—and loved—all four of us. But our preacher dad was Buster's favorite (after you read "Dust Bowl Days," G.H. Cummings's story on page 113, you'll understand when we say our dad was an animal whisperer). With his gentleness, attentiveness, and sense of humor, animals just took to him.

It was Daddy's idea to teach Buster tricks. We all got involved in the training and reward giving. Buster was a quick study. He learned to speak, sit, lie down, and roll over. He especially got praise and celebration when he rolled over, which he did with gusto. In fact, he was so motivated that when we said "sit," he just went ahead and did the whole routine, sit, lie down, roll over—in one fluid motion. Then, if the treat or praise wasn't forthcoming quickly enough, he'd *speak!*.

When it came to tug-o'-war, the Boston Terrier in him came to the fore. He would clamp his stubborn jaws on the rope or cloth, growl his tiny but determined growl, and never let go, even when we lifted him off the floor. He didn't have enough weight to pull the rope away from us, so he couldn't win that way. But he won by wearing out his opponent, because he never gave up.

In the neighborhood, especially with other dogs, his Toy Pinscher side was on display. An actual (big) Doberman

Pinscher resided in the house at the end of our street. Buster thought he was just as big as it was, and he tried to teach the Doberman a lesson about who was in charge of the neighborhood. That interchange didn't end well for Buster. It certainly didn't break his spirit; but it did teach him about his place.

During hot summers in a small town in rural Central California, we spent lots of time outdoors, riding bikes, playing in the vacant lot next door, swimming in the neighbor's pool, building forts, etc. Buster followed us almost everywhere. The goathead stickers were a bane in our summer bliss, and oh, how they hurt when they poked through our flimsy flip flops. Buster was tougher than we were. He'd get a sticker in his foot and not miss a step, but keep going on three legs. Once we even saw Buster continue his chase on only two legs! We exclaimed over his fortitude, then Cathy took pity and removed the stickers.

Daddy's fishing gear was in the garage where we sometimes played and where our neighborhood group of friends held our club meetings (calling ourselves the "Ninth Street Scavengers"). Buster would snoop around the garage while we played. One day he suddenly yelped and then cried pitifully. When we picked him up and looked closely, we saw he had gotten a fish hook stuck right through his poor little tongue. Well, this was horrifying.

We ran to find Daddy. Our kitchen table became an operating table, with we four girls (our friends Diane and Darlene from next door were there) trying to hold Buster while Daddy tried to pull out the hook (which had spurs, so it couldn't go back out the way it entered) with a pair of pliers. Buster didn't understand why it hurt so much and that it might have to hurt more in order to make it stop. He wasn't cooperating. Some of us girls were crying so we weren't much help, not wanting to be complicit in Buster's suffering, even though we wanted to end his pain. It felt hopeless. Finally Diane ran home and got her dad who was home that day. He held Buster firmly and fearlessly so Daddy could accomplish the delicate, painful, and slippery procedure. As soon as the hook had been pulled clean out of his tongue, Buster ran around barking and celebrating.

Sunday mornings were a whirlwind of squeezing our growing feet into church shoes, making sure socks matched, sashes were tied on dresses, hair combed, milk mustaches washed off, and Bible in hand to march next door for Sunday school, ready to greet, and be greeted by, the gathering church people.

One Sunday morning, when we were about eleven and twelve, our family was almost ready for church, when we heard a car horn honk and then brakes squeal. Then came a knock on the parsonage door. Someone sounded upset. We were used to all kinds of people and their crises coming to our door on a regular basis. But when we heard Mom exclaim, "Oh, no! Buster!," we came running. When we got there, Daddy was already carrying a limp little dog into the house, trying to hold him away from his Sunday suit, saying, "Get a towel!" Buster was stunned and whimpering. Daddy felt all his bones and determined nothing was broken. But there could be internal injuries. And we couldn't leave him alone. We never missed church unless we were *really sick*, and that may be the only time it happened. Daddy hesitated. But Mom said, "Well, the ox is in the ditch."

A few parishioners wandered over to the parsonage from the church next door, to seek the whereabouts of Rev. and Mrs. Cummings. A bit shaken, the preacher and organist finally arrived. Probably a few silent prayers were said for the charming, but sometimes problematic, four-legged PK. He recovered surprisingly well and learned that cars required at least as much respect as Dobermans.

Not long after that, Buster got very sick with Distemper

(dogs weren't always vaccinated in those days) and it was touch and go until he finally recovered.

You can be sure, when the time soon came for us to make another move, there was no question whether we'd take Buster with us to the new town. It was a town far up the north coast of California, in the Redwood country. We left hot, dry summers behind for ocean fog and wooded hills—and no goatheads!

The first school we attended there—a tall, imposing old building—had a long hallway that ran the length of the building, with classrooms on one side and auditorium, lunchroom, gym, and library on the other side. It was around the corner and one block from the parsonage.

Buster had a lot of freedom in this small town. He learned the lay of the land quickly, as he worked at keeping track of his people.

One school day, Beverly was in the school library, enjoying an opportunity to browse books and find something new to read. Lost in her private "book tunnel," she was at first unaware of the gasps and giggles of students closer to the door. Then she heard the *tick, tick, tick* of little nails on the linoleum floor. As they came closer, she turned from browsing shelves and saw Buster approaching! He did not seem surprised to see her, but was definitely happy. His little stub tail wiggled his whole rear end, and he demanded she pick him up.

When the time came to return to her classroom, Beverly thought, "What should I do with Buster?" He had obviously been enjoying one of his wanderings about the neighborhood. If she pushed him out the door, would he go home—or wander farther away? Probably the latter. So she carried him into the classroom, unsure of the reception they would get. Fortunately the teacher, Mr. Gilroy, tended to think the Cummings girls, PKs, could do no wrong.

To call this mustachioed, tweedy, absent-minded-professor-type eccentric would be an understatement.

As the other students reacted to Buster's arrival, Mr. Gilroy looked up from his desk and raised his bushy eyebrows over the top of his wire-rimmed glasses. "Beverly? Who is this?"

"Well, this is Buster. He's my dog! He just showed up and found me in the library!"

Buster's radar ears were taking in all the sounds of the somewhat chaotic classroom. He loved people, loved being held, and loved being near one of his personal humans. Mr. Gilroy just shrugged and agreed he could stay until lunch time. Buster got to wander around the room, greet other students, smell the plentiful eighth-grade smells. At lunch time Bev took Buster home. He never repeated this school trip. It seems one day of school was all he needed.

Buster was gregarious and had far more confidence than a 10-pound dog should. Sometimes that got him into trouble, but other times it gave him adventures! Buster Brown went to town more than once, and one of those times brought him to our church, which was only six blocks from the parsonage (almost everything in this small town was no more than six blocks from our home).

Buster was supposed to be in the house when we left for church. The pastor needed to get to church early! Buster seemed to understand. He usually curled up in a tight little ball on the couch when the go-to-church bustle began. But sometimes he managed to escape in order to play "catch me if you can" with all his humans. We would use all our methods: opening the car door and inviting him to jump in (occasionally worked), offering him a treat (often worked!), or even ordering him to come (seldom worked). Well, at least one time, we must have given up and left him outside.

In that Sunday evening service, congregational singing time was over (always a joyful time, with Mom playing the piano and everyone singing loudly and happily). As Daddy began to preach, we heard a noise. It was not a typical church noise. We girls always sat with our friends on the side of the church nearest the door. The noise was coming from the entrance door (wooden, not especially heavy). *Scritch! Scritch!* We glanced around. Did other people hear it? They seemed clueless.

Again, *Scratch! Scratch! Scratch!* This time more pronounced, more persistent. Buster. Had to be.

Beverly, closer to the end of the pew, got up as inconspicuously as she could and went to the back of the church. It was pretty difficult to be unnoticed when your dad is standing on the platform where he can see you, and your mother can always see you no matter where you are (at least it seemed that way). Slipping out the door, Beverly found our happy, wiggling little bundle of dog. Unlike school, Bev figured he would not be welcome in the church. Buster was profoundly disappointed when he was put into the family car (which was never locked) and he realized he would be staying there alone.

Slipping back into the church and returning to her seat, Bev whispered, "Buster was at the door!" A friend giggled, we glanced at Mom (who was intently listening to Dad) and we settled back into the service. Afterwards, we got to satisfy everyone's curiosity. Thereafter we were more careful to make sure our little escape artist was inside the house long before we left for church!

As part of a pastor's family, Buster was present for Christmas open houses, youth gatherings, missionary houseguests, and evangelists. Our denomination was organized into districts, with one minister overseeing all the churches in that district. At that time, the Superintendent of our

Northern California District was Dr. Z., a pleasant man, a good preacher, short and stout, and extremely outgoing. He was having Sunday dinner with us after visiting our church that morning. After Mom's excellent fried chicken with mashed potatoes and gravy, and chocolate cake, we settled in the living room for a visit. And Buster? He was, of course, in the middle of things. He and Dr. Z. were a little bit alike, short but super confident. Buster wanted to know this new person, who readily engaged him. At first, all was fine. Then the Superintendent leaned in and reached out to playfully "box" Buster's head.

We cringed and we wanted to blurt, "Don't do that!" But we felt inhibited by who this man was—Dad's boss.

Buster, who had never been played with roughly, wasn't particularly aggressive. He was a terrier, though, and could get overly excited. His eyes widened and his little stub tail stiffened. The good Dr. ignored these subtle signs and pursued the rough play, with another little cuff on Buster's side. That was too much. It was time for terrier discipline! Before anyone could stop him, Buster whipped round and sunk his teeth into the District Superintendent's hand!

A collective gasp was the only sound at first. Then came Dr. Z's exclamation of pain, Dad's "No, Buster!," and Mom's "Oh! What happened?" Buster retreated, not at all repentant.

The wound—not deep—was quickly tended to, the act was graciously forgiven, and we all could breathe again. Once again, our sassy, opinionated little terrier had taken center stage.

A short time later, the back porch needed repair on the parsonage, so a carpenter came to work on it. Buster, always present near the action, kept tabs on the carpenter's progress. A board was leaning against the back of the house and something caused that board to fall and come whamming down with a great, sudden bang. Like a runner at the gunshot, Buster took off running. He must have heard a voice in his mind urging, "Run, Buster, run!" He ran the block to Main Street, then turned and ran up the center of town, past houses, store fronts, the theater, the gas station, the hamburger joint, the park, and kept going to the outskirts of town and on and on. When he came to his senses (in whatever sense a dog does that), he must have been exhausted, thirsty, disoriented, fearful, lonely, and lost.

We had no idea where he went. But someone who worked downtown and knew our family, called to say they saw our dog running up Main Street as if his life depended on it.

We knocked on doors and put up signs, with no results. Then one day a call came. Someone had found Buster, lost and exhausted, and had taken him in and cared for him. When a mutual acquaintance heard about it, they got us in touch. Buster was returned to his family! Happy reunion day! The prodigal, "problem" PK was welcomed home with great rejoicing.

About the time we left home for college, Buster's life (or "nine lives," if you will) came to an end. The District Superintendent (the one who forgave Buster for biting him) believed, some said eccentrically, that we will have our beloved pets with us in Heaven. We like to believe that also, and we smile to think what everlasting-life adventures await.

A WET-NOSED THERAPIST

by Gayle M. Irwin

Her blue vest spoke loudly to those who saw her. Children—at the bookstore, the library, or the school we visited—asked about the vest and what it meant.

"She's a therapy dog," I'd respond. And then I'd talk about how animals like her help people feel better.

Mary, a black and white Springer Spaniel mix, came into my family's life after the sudden death of her first owner. We adopted the seven year old from English Springer Spaniel Rescue's Rocky Mountain chapter in 2013. Her sweet disposition and calm demeanor made her the perfect therapy dog. She passed her Canine Good Citizen test and her Therapy Dogs, Inc. evaluation while living with her previous owner, and I continued her education and work by taking her to elementary schools, public libraries, nursing homes, and bookstores.

Her focus on and apparent empathy toward people's emotions made Mary an incredible therapy dog. She easily tuned in to people experiencing sadness or loneliness.

Even at home, if she sensed my husband or I upset, she'd lay her head on one of our knees. Her brown eyes stared into our faces, as if saying, "It's all right—I'm here." Her compassion and kindness to us and toward strangers touched my soul, so much so that I bought a plaque and hung it on a wall in our home, to remind us that our four-footed friends play a major role in our happiness ... and in our lives.

The wooden sign says,

My therapist has a wet nose.

Those words are so true! Whether trained as a therapy dog or not, many canines possess that special sense which picks up on a person's mood. To people experiencing fear, grief, anxiety, unhappiness—dogs often respond with compassion through cuddles on the couch or heads on a knee. They bring comfort and they bring joy. Therapy dogs that visit hospitals and nursing homes help ease concern and loneliness. They bring smiles to faces, even in times when people don't feel like smiling.

A therapy dog knows when to be calm and when to be outgoing; Mary possessed both traits. She knew how to respond in different settings, approaching people at the library with an energetic springer wag or sitting quietly beside me in a classroom until instructed to "visit." People responded to her gentleness and affection.

Scientific studies show the simple act of petting a dog or cat calms spirits and lowers blood pressure, among other emotional and physical benefits. A therapy animal's gentle demeanor helps lessen anxiety and displays compassion.

God works that way, too. The Bible speaks about the love of God and the compassion of Christ. In Mark 6:34, we read, "When Jesus went ashore, He saw a large crowd, and He felt compassion for them because they were like sheep without a shepherd; and He began to teach them many things." Psalm 86:15 says, "But you, Lord, are a compassionate and gracious God, slow to anger, abounding in love and faithfulness." Compassion, love, slow to anger, faithful—characteristics of our Lord ... and most dogs. I saw those traits in Mary.

As I reflected upon the graciousness of God and the

kindness in this dog He had brought into our lives, I found myself examining my own life—just how compassionate am I toward others, including those who are difficult to be around?

I was challenged by this question, for I've worked with people who are not easy to like. However, I was reminded that each person experiences difficulties in life, and I cannot know all the troubles people experience, including those with whom I share an office. Therefore, I need to be less judgmental, less critical, less disagreeable in my dealings with whoever crosses my path—colleagues, friends, grocery store clerks, restaurant servers, and the person who cuts me off in traffic. I need to be compassionate and kind, despite the challenges in doing so.

Who can argue with God and the dog He's brought into our lives about showing compassion and kindness?

Mary's friendliness drew people to her. Her stub of a black tail wagged enthusiastically, her feet pranced, and her back end swayed as if to canine music. Those two-steps endeared her to people she met, and large grins replaced sullen pouts or disinterested expressions.

When I took Mary to the library or to the nursing home and she wore her blue therapy dog vest, she knew she had a job to do. She stopped by each person and nuzzled their hand as if to say, "I'm here now; everything will be all right."

Mary's wet-nose therapy positively impacted people's lives ... including my own. This sweet springer is no longer with us, dying of cancer in the spring of 2019, at 13 years old. However, her spirit lives on, and each time I gaze at that wooden plaque on the wall or come across a photo of her in a school or library setting, I smile. Her therapeutic personality remains in my heart and never far from my mind.

BRUNA

a poem by Alice Scott-Ferguson

BRUNA THE BEAUTIFUL DOG

Our Chesapeake Bay Retriever
with entrancing hazel eyes
more like a soul who could speak
who understood
more than food and fun
but measured the breath
of intelligence and traced
the space 'twixt dog and man
as though it were not, but built a bridge of love
and wove us as one!
So abounding in affection
The finest manners and inflection
of knowing
of showing
you knew
like few others
when and how to be aware,
to share silence
or space
a lick on the hand or face
compassion without ration
We did talk didn't we?
Of course we did!

You saw me weep
I heard your eyes speak
the morning you had to go
Were you really, merely a dog?
A dog that was a life-giving friend
or a friend who was a life-giving dog?

MAGGIE

by Dennis Ellingson

S ome years ago my wife, Kit, and I decided it was time to have a little dog as a companion. Our kids were grown and getting on with their lives. We used to have large or working dogs, so it was a little hard for me to consider something small. But when we visited our local humane society, they had just received a shipment of fifty pups! Out of this group was a sweet little girl who is part Papillion and part Long-haired Chihuahua. She was a year old and had lived in a kennel for a year. She looked at us and we looked at her, and we were all smitten. It was like God had placed us together.

After spending most of her life in a cage, Maggie wanted to go for a walk every day. Eleven years later, she is healthy and so are we!

We soon learned that Maggie is a natural therapy dog who takes to people who need some comfort, wanting to be near them. My dad, in Assisted Living, looked forward to Maggie's daily visits. She would cuddle up with him and help him calm down. When she sees an elderly person in a wheel chair, she instinctively wants to get up on their lap. She is especially drawn to people suffering with dementia.

Our favorite story is of a sweet couple we know. Rick and Lynnette are retired educators.

When we met, Rick had just retired from serving as a school superintendent. He was having some trouble relaxing. Soon after they pulled into the RV park where we were staying, we just all knew that God had placed all of us in each others' lives. The moment our new friend Rick and our dog Maggie laid eyes on each other, it was love at first site.

Rick is a very large and tall man and, for a time, played professional football. But, in reality, he is just a big teddy bear. So, here is nine-pound Maggie and 300-pound, 6'4" Rick spending time together. I call his large belly a shelf and Maggie likes to lie on that "shelf" on her back while Rick strokes her for, sometimes, hours.

We have all been friends for some time now, though as Snowbirds, we only see each other in the winters. But I think the great lesson here is how God gives us each other to love and share our lives. We pray for each other constantly and we miss each other terribly during the summer months. But one gift of God is that He has a way of putting the right people (and sometimes animals) together. Again, it is a great reminder of God's love for us. While at times He may seem distant, and we may feel lonely or sad, God is as close—or closer than—a friend.

Another sweet story about Miss Maggie: During the beginning of the Covid-19 pandemic, our church resorted to drive-in church. All the church members would drive their vehicles into the parking lot. With the sound system blaring we would sing, pray, and listen to Pastor Mike's message. Maggie loved to hang out the open window and listen. She seemed to be in a state of worship and very peaceful. I believe all animals that breathe do that to one degree or another. The Psalmist declares, "Let everything that has breath praise the LORD" (Ps. 150:6). Even the goldfish in your bowl, to squirrels in the trees and birds on the wing, must somehow give praise to their creator.

Jeanie Flierl with Beckett (p. 89)

Cathy Lawton as a child with
Amos (mentioned on p. 23)

OUR CATS

I and Pangur Ban my cat,
'Tis a like task we are at:
Hunting mice is his delight,
Hunting words I sit all night....
So in peace our tasks we ply,
Pangur Ban, my cat, and I....

–from a poem written by a Ninth-Century Irish monk

"Pet a cat when you encounter one."

–Jordan Peterson

BETTER THAN A GUARD DOG

by Jeanie Flierl

B orn and raised in the Milwaukee area, I set out on the adventure of a lifetime when I moved from Wisconsin to Colorado at the age of twenty-five. It was only myself and my cat, Beckett. I never considered myself brave or daring; I was a play-it-safe kind of girl. But the rugged Colorado mountains drew me like iron to a magnet to do something courageous. Never before had I experienced a sort of beauty that inspired me to become more than I was. Wisconsin may have Lake Michigan, but what could be better than skiing weekly in the mountains of Colorado instead of the hills of Wisconsin? This decision would test my entire being more than anything I had done before in my life. With my parents' reluctant blessing, I packed all my possessions in a small U-Haul trailer and headed west. Beckett and I would relocate to Denver.

Beckett was a seal point Siamese. The majority of his fur was light, with darker markings around his face, ears, feet, and tail. His eyes were beautiful, baby blue, and piercing. If you know Siamese cats, you know they are incredibly loyal, but to only one person. Beckett was a typical Siamese. Beckett may not have given me his blessing to a road trip and subsequent relocation. Still, he certainly gave his objection to car travel for the entire two thousand miles. Siamese have distinctive voices, more like a baby crying than a cat meowing. They like to vocalize as a greeting, a command, an objection, or an announcement. Frankly, traveling wasn't on his list of things he liked, and I have the mental scars to prove it. Even my attempts to mimic the comforts of home with the small litter box, water bowl, and food dish, didn't impress him in the least. However, anywhere his favorite human settled would ultimately be all right with him.

Once we arrived, I thought getting him used to a harness and a leash and taking him for walks would be quite fun. Wouldn't people think I was a great pet owner and think Beckett was an unusual cat? That would have been an excellent idea for a dog; not so much for a cat. He had other notions. If I held on to the leash, he would balk, claws full out on all four paws, heels dug in, legs stiff; but if I dropped the leash, he would walk next to me, dragging it. Silly cat. I didn't take him for many walks. But I did train him to sit for a treat. Sounds rather dog-like, definitely not cat-like. However, he would respond positively when his mood was right or if he was hungry.

After being in the south Denver area for a while, my second place to live backed up to a high school football field. The only time it wasn't dark and empty behind the duplex was on Friday nights during football season. Then it would stay bright until 10:00 pm or so; but I never went to bed before that, so it didn't matter.

One dark Saturday evening, a friend came over for dinner and to watch a movie with me. I fell asleep on the couch, and I only woke when she said goodbye and left. I got up and put on pajamas, unusual sleepwear for me when it was hot. I didn't think to lock the front door, which was left unlocked since my friend left. I just went to bed.

In the early morning hours, I was awakened by low, guttural growling under my bed. Yes, cats can growl, which could mean annoyance, fear, anger, or aggression. In the ambient light that entered through the bathroom window,

I saw the silhouette of a man standing in my bedroom doorway. Keeping my eyes on him, I reached and turned on the light beside the bed. I quickly obeyed his stern command when he said, "Turn it off." In the few seconds the light was on, though, it illuminated a young man in a dark hoodie. His hood hid most of his face, but I thought I saw bloody scratches on his cheeks. Beckett continued his angry growl.

Without thinking, I got out of bed, thankful I had chosen pajamas, and shouted, "Get out!" When he turned around, I proceeded to push on his back. Because I knew how high my hands were when I shoved, I could later tell the police how tall I thought he was. The young man was probably as surprised to hear a feisty girl yelling at him as I was to find a man in my bedroom. As I pushed him, he asked if he could leave by the backdoor. I knew he had come in by the unlocked front door, and I kept shouting no, he would leave by the door he had entered. Beckett continued his growling until the door firmly closed behind the intruder. With weak knees, I quickly locked the door.

In total relief, I sprinted to the kitchen and called 911, and then sat on the couch, waiting for the police to arrive. Beckett, realizing the danger had passed, sat on the couch next to me, purring his usual, comforting purr. I sat petting him, crying, and saying over and over, "Thank you, Lord, thank you, Beckett. Thank you, Lord, thank you, Beckett."

When the police officer arrived, I let him in, and Beckett didn't growl. He knew if I invited someone in, he didn't need to go into protection mode. I have no doubt that my fifteen-pound cat, with claws that could dig into concrete to stop himself from being led on a leash, would have used those lethal weapons on anyone who tried to touch me. The police officer's supposition was that this young man had gotten into a fight and was looking for a place to clean up before he went home to face his parents. Of course, we would never know for sure.

That week Beckett, my guard-cat, had his five minutes of fame. He got an article written about him in the *Littleton Independent* with the headline, "Woman's Cat Awakens Her to Intruder." My protective cat became famous, and I became more diligent in my own safety. Needless to say, I never again forgot to lock the door. Thank you, Lord. Thank you, Beckett. You were better than a guard dog.

BOB
An Angel At My Doorstep

by Nancy Swihart

I softly called into the darkness, "Bob, are you there?" An orange head popped over the screen door's grate, and big yellow eyes peeked at me. Bob was there. Always.

This little routine helped to keep my soul from fracturing during a difficult time in my life.

During those first post-op days, the couch in the living room encapsulated me. Severe anxiety and pain had replaced any sense of God's presence.

No matter my distress, my mind told me God was there. But that knowledge did nothing to change the pain the surgery had inflicted on my psyche and body. A post-traumatic response from childhood surgery had caught me by surprise, and I suffered from anxiety that tormented me day and night.

During the day, when my husband, Judd, was home, he was my anchor that I turned to for reassurance of God's tangible presence. At night, while Judd slept, Bob filled the gap. I spent the nights that warm spring in the living room on my makeshift bed. The door, just a few feet from the couch, led to the front porch, and Bob, desiring to be as near as he could to a human being, made his home on that porch.

While the rest of the world slept and I did not, I would

call out, "Bob, are you there?" Immediately, he would run to the screen. Ah, I was not alone. His instant response, his soft meow as he peered in at me, became the physical presence I needed to remind me all was well with the world, that life is normal, concrete, and loving.

Bob had gone through his own traumatic experience just a few months earlier.

I remember Opa (what the grandchildren called their Grandpa Judd) coming back into the old farmhouse after the grandkids had left one day.

"Well, the children found a new friend today," he quipped. I had a distinct sense he was somehow relieved. "A kitten wandered out of the woods and into the front yard while they were here. It must have heard them playing. I told them to go ahead and take it home before Oma [the grandchildren's name for me] saw it and adopted it." Then Judd added, "All we need is another cat."

Thus, Bob (short for bobcat) went to live and be loved across the road and down the gravel drive. After leading a happy kitten life, loved by our six grandchildren, he grew up to become a mature, loving, but prowling tomcat.

Numerous cuts, scratches, and abscesses over time began to threaten Bob's happy existence. But he was unique among all the other farm cats where he lived. Despite his new adventures, he remained a loving, playful, gentle cat devoted to the family.

The children's parents finally made a difficult decision. Contrary to their usual practice, they would invest in this farm cat that everyone had grown to love. They would take him to the vet to cure his wandering spirit.

Besides doing the necessary surgery, the vet treated Bob's sores and bathed and groomed him.

Somehow, after all those indignities, the meek, sub-missive Bob changed his allegiance. Once home, and as soon as the carrier door opened, Bob ran away from home up the gravel drive and across the road ... back to where the story had begun. No matter how many times the children would come to get him from my front porch, Bob would return to Grandma's nonthreatening refuge.

I deny the accusation of secretly feeding Bob. He may have eaten with my other cats, but I swear I never tried to entice him away from my grandchildren.

It took Bob a while to convince everyone that he was at home with Oma. Whatever the logistics of Bob's departure from the grandchildren, I thank God for the angel that I believe He sent to my doorstep to accompany me through one of my darkest valleys.

It did not take Bob long to become a staunch and dedicated member of my menagerie. When we built a new home and moved across from the farmhouse, Bob quickly accepted his new digs. In the summer, he stood guard on the porch divan; in the winter, along with Missy and Oreo, our original kitties, he claimed a cozy warm box in our insulated, attached garage. Life was good.

One day, however, Bob took an unplanned detour from this peaceful existence. I had a ritual at this new home. Every morning as soon as I got up, I would go to the garage and feed the three cats their breakfast. One snowy morning, after Judd had left for work, I missed my orange friend. Finding it a little strange, I calmed myself by thinking that maybe he had gone across the road to the barn to find shelter.

No Bob at lunchtime, however. And the snow contin-ued falling into the afternoon.

By late afternoon, the snow stopped. With five inches of snow, sleds, and a made-for-sledding yard, Sara and her boys chose to have extended home school to "study the art of fun." Seeing them from my kitchen window, I stepped out on the front porch to watch. On his way home from work, Judd had also stopped his truck to watch the sledders.

The threesome stopped to go over to the truck to say "hi" to Opa when they heard a mournful "murow."

"Dad, it sounds like there is something under your truck. Did you run over a cat?" asked Sara. She and the boys immediately began to walk around the truck, looking under tires (could have caught its tail), under the hood, under the bed. Nothing. But as soon as they talked, the pitiful mews began again.

"Mom," Sara called to me across the road. "There is a cat somewhere in Dad's truck, but we can't get it to come out."

"Oh," I shouted back. "I'll bet it is poor Bob!"

Recognizing familiar voices for the first time all day, Bob had found enough courage to call out from what had been a warm hiding place but had become a cold, wet, day-long prison.

Failing to entice him from under the truck, Judd drove home and into the garage. Finally, down out of the cold, dirty, muddy truck bed crawled a chagrined, wet, and dirty Bob.

Country Bob, who had huddled all day in the parking lot at work, listening to the strange sounds of city life, not daring to make a sound as the snow fell and people swarmed around the truck.

Wise Bob, who knew that silent suffering could save his life.

Smart Bob, who never again slept under the bed of the truck.

My Bob, an angel who came to my doorstep and stayed to be my joy.

TAKING IN STRAY CATS

by Dennis and Kit Ellingson

Elmo was the friendliest cat we ever had. We saw him hanging out at the park in Klamath Falls, Oregon. He was abandoned but had fared well with handouts from people's picnics. A family in the park asked if we would take him home. We decided to do it. He was so nice, big, and friendly.

Soon we moved to the little village of Tiller, high in the mountains of Southwest Oregon. We used to talk about the place as "ten miles past nowhere." I served as pastor of a small church there. The church board built us a nice new parsonage where once a berry patch and orchard had been.

People joked that Tiller had more Black Bears than people. Once we had a mother bear and her cubs climb into our apple tree out back. She was huge and evidently hungry. We were concerned that she might break into our little house. But what interested her was the apple tree. It was fall, and the apples were ripe. She climbed into the tree and shook it for hours until every apple was tossed. Then she and the two cubs ate them all!

Anyway, ole Elmo was so friendly, everyone and every creature was his friend. Come fall, the bears, foxes, raccoons, and skunks came walking down their old path in search of the old, familiar berry patch and orchard. Of course the berries and fruit trees were now gone, and our house sat there instead. Elmo was so friendly that he would go out to greet even the wild animals. He just wanted to say hi and play with whoever wanted to play. He was afraid of no one, and they all seemed to like him very much. The Black Bears came in shades of black, red, and brown. Elmo made friends with them all.

Elmo, like Jesus, reminds me to be a friend to everyone, even when they seem a bit wild or just are not very nice. I have developed the habit of seeing everyone as a friend. I want to talk with them, find out about them, and often I pray with them.

Telly was another stray cat that befriended us. Our son, Todd, said the little cat had followed him from school. But he told a little fib because he actually carried him home. While we were living in Vancouver, Washington, we moved into a house that had not been lived in for some time. It was a nice old house but the back lawn and trees were overgrown. Blackbirds had taken up residence and when we went out, they would bombard us. Of course that was very scary for our kids. Telly helped us out. As the birds dove at us, he would jump high in the air and grab at them until they finally flew away. It was his way of being helpful.

THE CAT WE LEFT BEHIND

by Jacob Stern
as told to Susan Bulanda

Life in Belgium was not bad when I was a child. We had a nice house and a loving family consisting of my parents, a brother, a sister and myself. We also had a very funny cat. This cat loved to play and would chase a string and entertain us for hours at a time. I especially enjoyed it when the cat would sit next to me as I read a book. He would slowly close his eyes and blink, his way of letting us know he was happy and contented. Each member of the family had a unique relationship with him.

But World War II changed our lives drastically. There were families that would disappear, or the father of a family would not return. There were rumors that Jews were being sent to camps to do work, or as we suspected, to be killed.

The tension was mounting as more and more people were taken. Then one day the Germans told my father that he was to report to "work" in Germany.

My father gathered our family together and told us, "I want each of you to gather a small suitcase of clothes. We are going to hide in Brussels to get away from the Germans."

This was because my father suspected that his work assignment in Germany was not real and that he and all of us would be sent to the camps and killed.

We had to do this very quickly and not look obvious. So we were forced to leave everything except a few personal items.

As we were getting ready to leave I asked my father, "What about our cat? We cannot leave him behind."

Father said, "We have to look as casual as possible so that we do not cause suspicion. We must look like we are just going to visit relatives. We cannot take the cat."

I understood the need to look like a family on a casual outing. But the most heart wrenching of this episode was that we had to leave our beloved cat.

All of us cried because we were afraid for the cat, but my father promised that once we were all safe, he would send a truck back in a few days for some more of our stuff, including the cat.

A few days later, we learned that when the truck arrived at our house, the Gestapo had already discovered that we ran into hiding and sealed our house. Our neighbors told us that the Germans had loaded everything into two trucks and taken it away.

We never found out what happened to our cat. All these years I have hoped that he escaped while the Germans were loading our stuff into the trucks and that someone adopted him.

Fortunately, all of my family survived. But we never forgot our cat.

Dennis Ellingson's grandson
on Bubba (story on p. 141)

Beverly Coons riding
Wyndham (story on p. 110)

Marilyn Bay with one of her lambs
(her stories start on p. 127)

OUR FARM ANIMALS

"The ox knows it owner and the donkey its master's crib."
–Isaiah 1:3

"A good man takes care of his animals."
–Proverbs 12:10

"Farmers farm for the love of farming. They love to watch and nurture the growth of plants. They love to live in the presence of animals. They love to work outdoors."
–Wendell Berry

MY "HEY, SHEEP"

by Nancy Swihart

Rex was gone. After several long weeks of incapacitating weakness, my "Hey, Sheep" had finally died.

Rex, his given name, had come to live at the farm to be a companion to Arabella, the "defective" ewe that was living out the rest of her life on the farm. Rex was a big sheep, well over two-hundred pounds. I was the one person who could approach him without fearing his ram-like aggression. Supposedly a wether when we bought him, we slowly discovered that (is there a biblical axiom of "you can judge a ram by his fruits"?) he had never been totally stripped of all his male accoutrements. No one who had been knocked down by Rex would vouch for the success of that de-ramming. In fact the last shearer had carried bruises for over a week after finding Rex's "ramness" too much to wrestle to make it worth another shearing.

Every summer after that shearing fiasco, I took pity on Rex. My father-in-law had purchased a pair of hand shears for me, so on a particularly hot day I would dig out those old shears and head for the sheep pen. Sitting on the bench of a picnic table, with Rex's collar tightly grasped in my left hand, I would snip away at the deep, thick coat of wool. He seemed to enjoy those interludes of my undivided attention. My shearing attempts went only as far as Rex would allow me to go, which meant that I could do his back and sides, but definitely not his belly. Thus, every summer, when all the other neighboring sheep ran around trim and clean, Rex sported a long skirt that hung from his midsection to the ground. He never had to suffer the humiliation of the other sheep who had been stripped naked. At least that seemed to suffice as an excuse when other sheep owners raised their eyebrows at my shearing expertise.

After Arabella died, I put our miniature donkey, Sandino, in the sheep pen with Rex. Rex greeted this companion with bruising and ramming. In desperation I let him run with the two horses for a day, thinking they would intimidate him into submission and gentleness, but I quickly decided I might have some serious vet bills to pay if the horses continued in the same vicinity as Rex. So Rex became master of his own domain—lonely, but in control.

He also had lost all invitations to be a part of our living nativity. Every year we host about two-thousand people who walk through the guided tour of what we call Bethlehem Revisited. After I sold my flock of sheep, we trailered in a flock from Kansas State. We had tried Rex as part of the borrowed flock joining the shepherds "out in the fields." Not a joiner, however, he was quickly rejected from that role. Next, we tried tying him at the manger with Mary, Joseph, and baby Jesus. Tied far enough away that he could not harm the sleeping baby, unfortunately he was close enough to carefully gauge a sneaky jab at the back of the magi's knee which sent the unsuspecting wiseman solidly to the ground. So, once again Rex became just background noise with his occasional unique "baa" (which sounded more like a rumbling, deep burp) as the group walked past his pen.

It was after ostracizing him to a distant pen that I began to call him "Hey, Sheep." In the mornings and evenings as I exited the kitchen door to do my feeding chores, Rex would begin to call to me. And I would respond, "Hey, Sheep." It became our little ritual. After months and years of doing this, I almost forgot that his name was Rex.

And now, after years of residency on the farm, "Hey Sheep" was beginning to falter. He had long passed the age that most sheep live. For weeks he hadn't been able to stand for long, and when he fell could not get up without help. I would tug and pull on his wooly, 200-plus pound body, lifting him up until he could get his feet planted securely under himself. As he wobbled to find his balance, I would slowly walk away hoping that this time he would gather the strength he needed to keep going.

I gave him glucosamine, tried to make his pen free from anything that would trip him, and held my breath, waiting for him to get better. Each morning when, after getting him stabilized the night before, I went out to feed the other animals I would find him lying helplessly on his side. As soon as he heard my voice, he would begin to struggle to get to his feet, his legs striking the air in frantic movements. And once again I would go to his pen and struggle to get his feet planted back on the ground.

My energy dipped, and my anticipation each morning began to be replaced with a heavy sense of dread. Coming round the side of the barn I would let my gaze sweep to the far south of the barnyard, up the slight hill of the sheep pen, and fall upon (oh, blast it!) the wooly, white mound with legs pumping fruitlessly against the air.

I finally decided to let nature take its course. I knew that animals, particularly sheep and horses, cannot survive if they don't get up. I felt that maybe it was my encouragement that kept him alive. Maybe, if he did not hear my voice, he would give up and die. Maybe that would be less cruel than keeping him alive. So … for two days I whispered when I was outside so he could not hear my voice. When I fed the other animals, I stayed far away from the sheep pen. Yes, he was down. No, he was not moving.

The morning of the third day I worked up the courage to go to his pen. Slowly walking up to his body, I whispered, "Hey Sheep." To my dismay, his legs began pumping and he threw back his head to look for me.

I have always felt that one of my strongest callings has been to be a caretaker of God's creatures. It is a deep-down kind of calling that, were I to turn my back on it, I would be denying a huge part of my very essence, something that has defined my soul. So when I am faced with failure in that caretaking, when I bump up against this fallen world that faces the curse of death, I am forced to recognize that we are not home yet. Nor are our animals.

Not able to watch my sheep go through any more suffering, I finally called our country vet. I led her to where Rex lay and watched as she listened to his heart (fine and strong), his breathing (regular, lungs clear). No problems there, but obviously he would not survive long in his prone condition. With gratitude I watched as she administered the shot that would ease him into oblivion.

As we walked away from his limp body, finally at rest, I mourned the loss of another one of my friends and I recalled a plaque that my mother had bought for me when I was a teenager:

The friends of my childhood
Were mostly stray cats,
Or poor homeless dogs
All forlorn.
I wonder where now
Are their dim trusting souls,
Those friends whom
I still faintly mourn.

To the list of my cats and dogs, I have added sheep, horses, donkeys, cows, and now a goat—all of whom are my friends.

I like the picture that C.S. Lewis paints in *The Great Divorce* when he portrays a character named Sarah Smith from Golders Green. Lewis gives us his own attempt at trying to understand the role that human beings may have as caretakers of God's creatures. In *The Great Divorce*, the narrator is being guided through the foothills of heaven by his old mentor, George MacDonald, when wonderful expectation fills the air. A procession of joyful bright spirits comes out of the distance, followed by boys and girls singing, all preceding a lady in whose honor all this is being done. Her face shines with unbearable beauty. The narrator relates that following the lovely lady were cats, "dozens of cats. And all those dogs ... why, I can't count them. And the birds. And the horses."

When the narrator queries his guide, MacDonald explains:

> "They are her beasts. ... Every beast and bird that came near her had its place in her love. In her they became themselves. And now the abundance of life she has in Christ from the Father flows over into them. ... It is like when you throw a stone into a pool, and the concentric waves spread out further and further. Who knows where it will end?"

Hey Sheep had his own quirky, cantankerous personality. But he was one of God's creatures, and I had become his devoted caretaker. With that caretaking came responsibility, but also joy and, in a sense, worship of the Creator who had placed him here in this little patch of farmland that I call home.

WYNDHAM
The Gentle Giant

by Beverly Coons

A fter my husband died, my animals helped me through the grief, loss, and life adjustments. I told you about my Rottweiler who was such a "bad girl" that she provided distraction therapy (see page 44). Thankfully, I had another, more gentle, animal therapist in my life. Wyndham was a 1300 lb., 16.3 hand chestnut horse. That description does not do him sufficient service. He was the childhood dream that came true at the age of 47, the gentle giant, my sweet baboo. Wyndham, whose very presence brought me comfort and peace, helped ease the pain of losing Curt. He was a soothing therapist.

He had some unique mannerisms that always made me laugh. Wyndham lived at a horse boarding facility, but I came to give him his special meal each night. He evidently knew the sound of my truck. People at the barn told me he would begin his routine as soon as I drove up. And there he would be as I came to retrieve his feed tub, tossing his head up and down and voicing his impatience with a strong series of *huh, huh, huh*s. He would not stop to greet me. I had a job to do first. Finally the feast was presented. He was very mannerly. I would say "Get back, Wyndham!" and he would move away and stand until I said "Okay." Then he would rush to the bowl, thrust his big head in the wet mess, and *then* decide it was time to greet and thank Mom. With food dripping everywhere, he would turn and nuzzle my shoulder, or face. I never left the barn clean!

I taught Wyndham to kiss. There's no therapy quite like a Wyndham kiss! A horse must have an affectionate personality to learn to kiss—and a great greed for horse treats. I would stand on his right side and expose my stash of treats, giving the command: "Give me a kiss, Wyndham." And then I would wait. Finally, his impatience for a treat would get him to nudge me with his nose. I would proffer my cheek (cautiously) and keep repeating the kiss request. It amazed me the first time he actually twisted his large hairy lips towards my cheek and landed a major horse kiss! Lots of treats. Ask again. Another none too delicate kiss. He got so good at it, he would offer kisses while we were walking together, or when I was standing next to him, talking to someone. And he would share a kiss with anyone courageous enough to stand in the appropriate position, offer a treat, and ask. When a 1300-pound horse swings his big head at you, parts his large lips and pushes them against your cheek, it's impressive.

By the time Wyndham was 29, he was plagued with a variety of physical problems: arthritis in his upper neck, Cushings Disease, and teeth loss. Gone were trail rides, jumping little jumps, and gallops in the field. Now we had "picnics" in the field with easy-chew horse treats, and lots of grooming. Sometimes I just leaned on him and talked to him while he grazed.

One day I had brought Wyndham in for his dinner, and I decided I just *had* to get on him again. He'd been diagnosed as ataxic (lack of coordination in movement, due to the arthritis in his neck), and I had been advised not to ride. I threw caution to the wind that day, found my helmet (kept a little caution), and led him into the arena. I climbed up on the arena fence as I had many times in the past when riding him bareback, and swung my leg over his lovely broad back. Ah! Home again.

Wyndham responded immediately to my nudge and cluck, and moved off in his surprisingly big walk. Ears pricked, eyes bright, his whole body shouted, "We're goin' for a ride! Me and my mom are workin' together again!" Funny old man. I actually had to put a little pressure on the halter to make sure he didn't break into a trot! It did not become a daily event; but occasionally, when he seemed stable, I repeated the little amble around the arena.

But owning Wyndham had become so much more than riding. He had become a companion, an equine friend, and one of my special therapists.

Wyndham is gone now. There are still horses in my life, but not owned by me, and not my Windy Bindy. Both my dog Grace and my horse Wyndham were once-in-a-life-time companions. But then, aren't they all? Each is unique; each pours something into our lives that makes us richer, better. Thank you, God, for the gift of our animals.

DUST BOWL DAYS

by G.H. Cummings

When we moved to the farm in St. Francis, Kansas, in about 1933, we found it run down. In fact the land was a veritable dust bowl. The wind had blown the topsoil and piled it along the fence so high, it had nearly buried the fenceposts. There were Russian Thistles everywhere. A big, wild plum thicket had grown up in back. A few rusty pieces of farm machinery were nearly buried in weeds.

Having arrived nearly destitute—Daddy, Mama, my twin sister Catherine and I, and our younger sisters, Carolyn and Dottie (our youngest sister, Martha, would later be born in the farm house)—we started out farming with one cow, a few chickens, a pig, and a borrowed team of horses. Most machinery was borrowed. But during the first year, Daddy managed to get the crop in, start a kitchen garden, and bring a semblance of order to the farm. We soon were able to buy our own team of horses, Topsy and Bess, small black mares. Bess was high strung and Topsy was laid back, a plodder. Quite a team.

On the farm, my three sisters and I had so much room to run, so many things to observe. Coyotes howled in the night and once in a while we would sight one. You could hear pheasants in the distance, and many, many birds. A pair of mockingbirds would migrate in each spring and make their nest in the mulberry tree. We seemed to always have a cat around. It was a real circus to see those mockingbirds dive bombing that poor cat. She could hardly walk across the yard. And we loved their melodious music. I remember thinking that they were singing all the bird songs they had learned down south in the winter time.

Every day, as soon as we got home from school, it was chore time. We would raid the cupboard, where Mama had saved the leftover cocoa from breakfast, or get a slice of bread, anything, and then on to the barn. I'd go out to get the cows, which could be quite a walk, then put them in the barn, and feed them in their stalls. Carolyn and I would do the milking. Dottie would come later and milk her one cow, a very gentle Holstein. We'd take the milk to the house, and Cathy would cool it in the pump house. The cold well water would bring the temperature of the milk down as she stirred it. To the rhythm of the stirring she would sing, either a church song or the latest pop song of that day.

I would take the rest of the milk into the barn and separate it—a big job for a young boy.

One day Carolyn was finishing milking the last cow. It was a little Jersey, who had a bad habit of switching her tail around right into your face. Her tail usually had a few cockle burs in it. And she would try to put her foot into the bucket of milk. Carolyn got all she could take one day and gave the little cow a shove. She soon came running to the house exclaiming that the cow was in the manger!

We ran to the barn. When we walked in, all we could see was four feet sticking up out of the manger. We got ropes and worked feverishly, and she came out in time. Daddy explained that a cow would die very quickly in that position.

I mentioned our pig. We would sit on her, pretending to ride her. In the evenings she would go in and out, bringing mouthfuls of straw and piling them in the corner. Grunting contentedly, she would snuggle in her pile of straw for the night.

One day we came home from school to find she was gone. We learned that Daddy had butchered her that day! Heartbroken, we kids informed our parents that we would not eat any of that meat! And we didn't. Daddy sold it to some people in town who loved pork, not a pig.

I came home from school one day to find two new horses. They were big blacks, larger than the original two. We were really coming up in the world. I needed to disk the field, so I hooked up the new horses with two old-timers. Everything went fine. When I came in with the team from the field, Daddy had arrived home.

He looked at the team and his face blanched white. He asked if I'd been disking with them. I told him yes. Then he told me that the new team had not been broken, ever. Not even halter broken! I had gently got them in the stalls, found harnesses to fit, put bridles on them, bits in their mouths, then hooked them up to one of the most dangerous pieces of machinery on the farm.

They worked perfectly and always did as long as we had them. My favorite, Old Blackie, got sick a couple of years later. He was down and couldn't get up. The vet told us he had brain fever. Daddy said we'd have to put him down and bury him. I pleaded with him to let me feed Blackie and see if he would get better. Surprisingly, he let me.

Each morning and evening I would take food and water to him, then help him eat and drink. He would whinny when I approached. It was hard to let him go, and it got harder as the days went by. But finally we had to dig that huge hole and bury him.

Our other horses were Prince, Bessie, and Topsy. After Old Blackie died, my favorite was Prince. A gelding, he was half Morgan. This gave him his big feet. He was a fine riding horse in spite of his feet. The neighbor boy had a fast pony. He would try to race me. Prince would take a while to get his big feet going, but when he did, he always won! One time I slipped off his back. I always rode him bareback, since I didn't have a saddle. He was running when I fell off. I didn't need to be afraid of him stepping on me. He stopped instantly! He stood stock still until I could get up and get back on.

I could get on him in the pasture without a bridle, and say "Get the cows," and he would go after them and bring them to the barn. I loved Prince.

Bessie was a different story. One day she pulled a good one on me. I was bending over in the manger in front of her. She must have opened her mouth wide and bit down hard. She had a mouth full of straw hat and my hair. I yelled and she let go. When I raised up, I thought she had a very amused look on her face.

Then there was Topsy, who was bad about kicking. If I walked suddenly into the barn behind her, she would kick me, not terribly hard, but it did hurt. Another trick she had was standing on my bare foot. The more I yelled, the harder she pressed. My foot was sore for a week.

One day Carolyn came into the house and announced that she had helped a little chicken to be born! Our parents asked her how she did that. She said she broke the shell and let the little chicken out.

"The little chicken will die if you do that," our parents said. And it did.

I don't know where he came from. But one day a male pigeon arrived at our farmhouse. He loved to sit on the sill of the open window. We would nudge him on his side. He would fight us with his wing crying *lookity coo, lookity coo*. Daddy loved to play with him when he came in from work.

Another mysterious visitor was Caw Caw, the talking crow. He just showed up one day. He would ride around on Daddy's shoulder, talking all the time. He'd say "Hello," but the rest of his talk we didn't understand. When we walked down into the pasture or field, he would fly along beside us, landing on the fence posts and jabbering. He was a lot of entertainment. Then one day in a storm, he flew into the blades of the windmill. Another sad reminder of the temporal state of affairs on the farm.

When Daddy found an abandoned nest of pheasant eggs in the field he put them under our little Bantam hen who was forever wanting to set. She hatched them out! We loved to watch the tiny pheasants as she clucked them along the garden rows, looking for insects. And it was great entertainment when they got a little older and would run down the rows as fast as they could go with the little mama hen squawking, flapping her wings and running after them. They ran off one day and we never saw them again.

We were in school one spring day when a dust storm was so bad the sky became dark, as dark as the darkest night. We were all told to go home. The kindly principle drove my sisters and me home in his car. He drove slowly with his headlights on, barely able to see the road.

In those days, we could look at the sky and tell by the color which way the wind was blowing. If the color was red, it was a south wind coming from the Red River Valley in

Oklahoma. If it was black, it was blowing down from the Black Hills of North Dakota!

Rain storms were very welcome things! It was usually hot and dry. When the rains came, we kids would run out in the yard and dance around, holding our faces up to the rain. The smell was wonderful.

One afternoon I went down in the pasture to get the cows for milking. I rode my old bicycle. I don't think Johnny the bull liked my bicycle. Anyway, he charged me, knocking me and the bike down. Then he began to gore me the best he could without horns. My twin sister, Cathy, came running down into the pasture, carrying pitchfork, and chased off the bull. I think that was the sorest I've ever been in my life!

Another time, I had a team hitched to a trailer wagon that had a tongue and double trees on it. "Double trees" were what you hooked the horses up to. There was a down grade where I was working. When the horses lunged forward, I lunged for the lines, tripping and falling behind them. I held on to the lines to try to slow the horses down. Their back hooves were very close to my head. I was on my back under the front axle of the trailer. It was bumping against my chin. I thought if I let go, the axle might take my head off! Well, I yelled. And guess what, again my twin came running. She stopped the horses and got me out of there. That was the second sorest I've ever been!

Mama carried large buckets of feed out to the chickens daily. We kids often gathered the eggs. One hen would peck us if we tried to reach under her and get the eggs from the nest. It always tickled Mama when a hen would get in the house through an open window and lay an egg on her bed. One time a hen laid an egg on the washing machine.

When a dust storm began to blow upward, Mama

would be out running after the hens with their little chickens, gathering them up in her apron and bringing them to safety.

In high school, I wanted to play in the band. Our music teacher, Phil Moore, taught a group of us to play recorders, then encouraged us to get band instruments. When the dealer came to our school, I picked out the trombone I wanted. The folks asked how in the world would I pay for it. Then an idea struck me.

Besides the large flock of white leghorns that laid white eggs, there were several colorful hens that laid brown eggs. I proposed that I would take the brown eggs to the market and sell them to make my payments. Daddy said that would be all right, though he didn't think there were enough hens laying brown eggs to do the job. But I persisted.

Well, I faithfully gathered my eggs each day and put them aside. Amazingly, it seemed we were getting more brown eggs than ever! I would take them to the market and sell them to the grocer. Then I would go to the post office, buy a money order, and send it to the music company. I never missed a payment—though I'll admit, I missed a few notes on my trombone.

WHAT CHARLENE TAUGHT ME

by Millie Bay

The soft sound of bleating reached me as I sauntered toward the chicken house turned lambing barn. We had acquired the old, egg-producing chicken shed, a long, low dilapidated building with windows all across the front; and remodeled it into a barn for our ewes at lambing time. There was room for nine individual pens (or "jugs") and one pen for supplies. Now, instead of the cackling of hens, the old structure was home to the bleating of sheep.

"Charlene! What a lovely baby you have," I exclaimed as I entered the sheep maternity barn on that freezing February morning. My nose wrinkled with the pungent odor of a full, moist barn. "But only one lamb this year? Usually you have twins."

Charlene had become one of my favorite ewes. In spite of the common thought that all sheep are stupid, she was quite smart. She was one of the "dead" sheep that my daughter Shelly and I had rescued from death on a scorching hot summer day several years earlier. She had been thrown out of a feedlot onto the "dead" pile, because she was so sick that the manager of the feedlot thought she was dead. We saw that she was still breathing, and with permission, brought her to our farm, where we nursed her back to health. She had recovered well and seemed to have no permanent problems. I decided to add her to my band of ewes. It was a good decision; she produced well for several years, often bearing twin lambs.

After bedding down Charlene and her still wet, white baby with lots of soft yellow straw, I proceeded to check the other mamas. Several more ewes had lambed, and each one had to be moved into an individual pen with her new baby/babies and made comfortable with straw, feed and water. I checked each ewe's bag to ensure she had an udder full of milk. Also, it was important to make sure that each lamb had figured out where to find its food supply and that each knew how to drink the thick warm colostrum which is so vital to a healthy start in life. There appeared to be a problem with one mother who had borne twin lambs. She had very little milk. I would need to keep an eye on these lambs to make sure they didn't starve.

Throughout the day, I entered the barn to the welcoming *baa baa* of hungry ewes. Little lambs echoed the cries of their mamas, but the plaintive cries of the two revealed that their tummies were nearly empty and they were starving. I checked all the other ewes and lambs; all seemed to be well with them. In a soft voice, I spoke to Charlene, "Charlene, you need to raise twins again this year."

I was certain the ewe that was short on "groceries" would not be able to feed both of her lambs. As a solution, I placed one of the new twins into the pen with Charlene and her new white baby. I gave Charlene the new orphan. This lamb was black. Charlene took one look and said, "Uh, uh, that's not my baby." I was sure she would change her mind in a little while, but by the time I figured there was no hope of reversing Charlene's mind-set, it was too late! Enough of Charlene's strong sheep smell, (an odor belonging to each sheep and detected only by other sheep) had infiltrated the black baby's body so that his birth mother would not take him back. On to the next plan I went. After putting a sheep halter on Charlene's head, I tied her on a fairly short leash in the corner of the lambing jug. She was given a small bucket of water and a flake of hay which she could reach; the short rope allowed her to lie down but limited her moving around. This way, she could not butt, nor smell the unwanted baby, and he would have opportunity to eat without being brutalized.

For several days, I monitored his eating and soon noticed that when it was time for the two babies to eat, Charlene would look lovingly to the left where her own lamb suckled, but when she glanced to the right side where the newcomer was eating, himself oblivious of any problem, Charlene would stomp her front foot and hop around on her back legs. As a general rule, ewes identify their babies by smell, but because of Charlene's limited range of motion there was no way Charlene could distinguish between the two lambs. There was only one answer: Charlene was not color blind! The little black lamb was a determined fellow and was able to get his meals even from an unwilling mother. After a few days, the smell of Charlene's wool and milk saturated his body so that he smelled just like her own lamb, and she decided to accept him as her own in spite of his being born to another ewe. I removed her halter and watched with delight as Charlene nuzzled the black baby as well as her own white baby—a family at last!

As I watched the new, happy sheep family, I thought about how often we as humans discriminate against some-one who is different from us. Like Charlene, we are happy with our own lives, and don't want to be bothered with any changes which might interfere with our contentment. There are so many different ways our prejudicial tendencies may manifest themselves, and it is certainly not always con-nected with skin color. I have been guilty of judging a person's actions as wrong. Maybe their choice of clothing, makeup or hairstyle seems inappropriate, or I don't agree with the way they express themselves. I am embarrassed to admit that, much like Charlene's unwillingness to accept a lamb different from herself, I have let my pettiness interfere with my willingness to accept and love people different from me. My goal is to let the love of God infiltrate me so thoroughly that I become color blind to the faults and differences of others.

NETTA AND THE SHEEP-PONY

by Millie Bay

I s it OK if we go out and ride the calves, Mom?" queried our oldest daughter. "We finished all our chores."

It was a lovely calf-riding morning on the Bay farm and the three daughters didn't want to waste any opportunity on such a day.

"Yes, but don't let Netta ride a calf. I don't want her to get hurt, and I don't think her folks would approve."

When our girls were young, my husband and I purchased our farm, believing it would be a wonderful place to raise our kids. The passing years confirmed that this momentous decision had been the right one. The three girls had chores to do and kept very busy, but they also had time, after they finished their work, for fun.

Some of that fun involved the four baby calves we bought to eventually provide both meat for our freezer and some to sell. Feeding the young black and white babies with bottles gave the girls extra opportunity to learn responsibility.

As the furry little calves grew, our girls decided it would be a challenge to ride them, just like they had watched cowboys ride bulls at the rodeo. Occasionally their younger cousin from the city came to visit for a few days. Netta loved the farm and all the animals that came with it—horses, chickens, rabbits, sheep, kittens, puppies, and of course, the calves. Wide-eyed she watched her "big" cousins mount the black and white calves, hanging on for dear life as the creatures bucked and kicked around the corral. We were thankful the girls never received serious injuries, though they inevitably were dumped on the ground.

Feeling left out, Netta begged, "Please let Netta ride, too. Netta wants to do it."

She was just too young; we couldn't take the chance of her being injured.

Finally, though, light donned! Why not capture a sheep for Netta to ride? With a much shorter distance to fall, she wouldn't likely get hurt. Thus began the saga of Sally the "sheep-pony."

After coaxing a large, fairly gentle ewe into the barn, we prepared her for riding. First, we placed a halter with a lead rope on her head. Next came a tiny saddle which we had purchased for our small pony years before. Carefully placing Netta on the saddle, we instructed, "Hang on to the saddle horn." Then, to avoid any surprises, we led Sally around the corral. Much to our surprise, Sally did not buck or try to dislodge her diminutive rider. She carefully carried her load as though she had given rides many times.

"See, Netta can ride," she joyfully exclaimed. Netta lost the desire to ride the "cow" after that. She had her own "pony."

In the fall we attended a small fair where our girls exhibited their lambs. We took Netta with us to the fair, and after the sheep show, there was a small-town parade. Since we had planned to let Netta ride Sally in the parade, we had brought all the riding paraphernalia. The parade began, and here came Netta riding her "sheep-pony." We again led Sally, but that was OK with Netta. She might as well have been riding a beautiful, golden stallion; she was so proud of her steed. How the parade watchers smiled and clapped as she rode by!

Decades later, Netta and my daughters still reminisce about Sally and the fun she provided all of us. We even have

a reminder, a photograph of Netta mounted on Sally holding the "reins" of her mighty steed and seated on a perfect,
albeit tiny, Western saddle.

RUN TO SAFETY!

by Marilyn Bay

On a brisk fall Sunday afternoon the phone rang. "Hi, Marilyn. Chris has got some cattle out. Any chance you might be able to help us get 'em back into his corral?" It was my friend Angie. She and my neighbor Chris were cattle people.

"Sure. Do you want me on foot or horseback?"

"Horseback would be good. When can you be there?"

"Should take me about thirty minutes to saddle up and ride over to Chris's place." I didn't often get to chase cattle horseback.

"OK. Get here as soon as you can. We're heading out now."

I pulled on a hooded sweatshirt and my heavy chore coat. I grabbed my winter work gloves then rushed out to the corral, the cold wind whipping at my face.

I haltered my trusty sorrel mare, Lady, and led her to the hitching post. I quickly ran a brush over her body to remove burs or other debris to prevent them from irritating her when I snugged up the saddle. Once saddled and bridled, I mounted and directed Lady toward my neighbor Chris's place, a little over a mile away.

Ten minutes later, I reached Chris's lane. He, Angie, and Angie's husband were trying to push a wild-looking black heifer toward the open corral gate, but she would have none of it. Whenever they got close to her, instead of moving away from them toward the gate, she would bolt past them and run down the pasture fence line.

Lady and I hung back, so that when the heifer bolted toward the fence line, we were there to dissuade her. Even with a fast, agile horse blocking her escape, the heifer refused to go through the open corral gate. Finally, the men had to take out a panel in the pasture fence, so that the heifer could rejoin the other cattle through a gate on the opposite side of the corral. Even then, she tried several times to break and run in the wrong direction.

We all let out whoops and hollers when the ornery heifer finally ran through the opening, and Chris slammed the gate behind her.

"Let me say how very glad I am to be a sheep gal," I told them, unable to resist the opportunity to jibe the panting cattlemen. "It took four intelligent stock handlers over an hour to get one bad-tempered heifer back into the corral. All I have to do if my sheep get out is call them, and the entire flock comes running home!"

They took my teasing in good humor. On my ride back home I thought more about the nature of sheep compared to cattle and other animals.

Sheep are skittish and virtually defenseless. They require very little persuasion to run back home to the sheep pen. Because of their vulnerability, sheep are very sensitive to danger. With one glance, even at a distance, the shepherd can tell if his flock is feeling threatened.

Not long ago I watched my neighbor's Toy Poodle cut across the back of my pasture. The next thing I knew, my entire flock of thirty ewes was high tailing it to the barn. Another time, I saw the ewes crowding into the loafing shed, an extension of the barn with one side open. Then I caught a glimpse of a coyote darting from behind the haystack on the far side of the sheep pen. The coyote was not in the pen and likely could not have gotten in, but the sheep were on high alert and crowded into where they felt safest, where they could take cover from the danger.

This is not such a bad lesson for people. *Help me, Lord, in times of spiritual danger to run into your protective fold.*

FRECKLES
The Faithful Farm Dog

by Marilyn Bay

How ya doin', boy?" Our all-purpose farm dog, Freckles, had come to meet me as I stepped outside one March evening, just before dark. "You're such a faithful boy, always here to help me with the chores." I dug my gloved fingers into his yellow, medium-length hair, still thick with his winter coat.

My companion charged forward, whining, then returned to me and catapulted into the air, directly in front of me. More whining.

"What's up, Freckles?"

Normally, during our walks to the barn, Freckles positions his head beneath my left hand for as much petting and scratching as possible. This evening, though, he continued his urgent, back and forth pattern, prompting me to hurry.

It was not the first time Freckles had alerted me to trouble. Several years prior, on a dark evening, he had scratched on our back screen door, a huge no-no, until I went outside to find that my horses had escaped and got into my garden. Another time he whined and ran back and forth, alerting me to a pack of coyotes in our pasture.

"What's wrong, boy? I don't see anything amiss."

All gates in the barn and pastures were shut, as the resting sheep chewed their cuds.

"You must be mistaken, Freckles."

Then out of the corner of my eye I saw a flash of brown fur. Freckles saw it, too, and darted after the bold coyote visiting the fenced area where my hay is stored. Freckles chased the intruder out into the field. The coyote was still running for its life when Freckles returned, wagging his tail and looking a little coy as if he wanted to say, "Can't you just trust me?"

"You are such a good boy, Freckles. You spotted danger even before the sheep did." I gave him an extended scratching and praise fest. "You're the best mutt a family could have."

Freckles's usefulness never ceases to amaze me. He is an odd mix of breeds: Yellow Lab, Sharpei, Heeler, and Border Collie. At least that is what the folks on the corner giving away puppies while the Fourth of July parade was getting ready to begin, told us. And I believe it. Who would make up such a claim?

At night, Freckles, so named for the brown dots on his nose, barks to keep coyotes at bay. He barks and runs out toward the intruders to send them packing, but he is also smart enough not to run too far out into the field when it is full of coyotes. He knows that he could be attacked and hurt or killed, should he allow himself to be lured too far from the barnyard.

Freckles is also a decent herder. He has learned to run out into the pasture when I say "Go get the sheep." Initially, he ran out and cut through the sheep, frightening and splitting the flock. By going out into the field with him, I was able to teach him to circle around the far side of the flock and push the sheep together toward home. Unlike finely-trained herding dogs that can place sheep where commanded with precision, Freckles' herding skills are limited to bringing in the flock at night. I believe that his shortcomings as a herder have more to do with my inability to teach him than his willingness to learn. Freckles is also very, very good at spotting trouble or finding missing animals. I've had stranded lambs out in the pasture, and he is able to find them, using his whine to signal me.

From the time I step out of the house until I go back inside, Freckles is either by my side or doing what I ask him to do. His constant presence is a comfort and help to me on the farm.

A PEACOCK FOR MOVING DAY

by Nancy Swihart

Watch out!" I pulled little Joshua out of the way as the men carefully eased the hide-a-bed couch through the front door.

Moving day! The culmination of planning and hard work. A move that I had both anticipated and resisted. Instead of starting, we were kind of, could I even say it, closing down.

Grandchildren, moms, and dads had joined us in transferring Judd's and my belongings across the road from our old home to the new one. In the kitchen, our granddaughter, Lillian, was unpacking dishes to put into the new cupboards. Her brother, Hezekiah, worked from his wheelchair as he filled the refrigerator with food from containers the men had just brought in. Each person had a job to do.

I glanced out the kitchen window at the home I was leaving. A sense of loss already filled my heart.

The farm had been my canvas for dreaming, holding unlimited possibilities for gathering people and doing ministry. Looking back over thirty years of living in that old farmhouse brought to mind the opening lines of one of my favorite poems: "It takes a heap o' livin' in a house t' make it home."

Yet, this home had not just been our livin' place. The farm had welcomed thousands of people into its acres as we offered camps, conferences, guided nativities, sunrise services, walking trails, and prayer trails.

The farm had been our offering to be used by God.

And now we were closing that chapter. My concern hung like a silent cloak around me. The new home was an empty slate. No history to build upon. A simple ranch-style home on a couple of acres and an old couple with faded dreams. What can God do with this place and with us?

Feelings and fears aside, I appreciated the wisdom of this decision. Our daughter and her family would move into the farmhouse and take over the responsibility of running the farm. They were young, energetic, capable. And we, the old couple, would move to our "retirement" home.

Our entire clan was whole-heartedly behind this project. Judd had spent many hours drawing up plans for our new dwelling. Our son Dan, who is artistic, helped beautify the project, while son-in-law, Dan T., an engineer, was Project Director. It was a perfect time for our teenage grandsons to gain skills that would last them for a lifetime as they worked alongside with their elders. They had worked for an entire year, evenings and weekends, to make this moving day possible.

While the men built, I packed and planned and fussed. Where would our furniture go in the new home? How would I decorate a ranch style when what I knew was old farmhouse decorating? Judd and I treasured the familiar antiques that had aged with us, so we had decided we would get nothing new. The old would work fine.

But I fretted and stewed. Would God bless this new home as he had the old one? Would I feel his presence as I had in every nook and cranny of the farm? Would this new home also provide a refuge, a place of solace, a reminder of God's presence to those who came to visit?

Leaving the grandchildren to finish their work in the kitchen, I stepped out onto the unfinished front porch. Everything was quiet as I gazed across our expansive new yard. For the moment, all activity must have been inside the house.

No one else was there to view what happened next.

There in the middle of an otherwise chaotic, busy day, I watched, dumbfounded, as a peacock stepped into view. A peacock. Not the usual crow, not a stray chicken from our neighbor's chicken coop. A peacock!

I stood transfixed. Immediately, my thoughts went back to my classroom. To most people, this might have seemed unusual but indeed not a sign. However, to this college English professor, it was a secret message from a God who knew my language of love so well.

I had taught the short stories of Flannery O'Connor in my American literature classes. O'Connor, a faithful Catholic, had a unique way of writing. As she would say, her stories showed the "action of grace in territory largely held by the devil." I taught my students to look for that symbol of grace, for that Christ figure, in the stories we read.

"Look for the symbol of Christ," I had directed my students as we plowed our way through one of O'Connor's short stories, "The Displaced Person." As with most of her stories, it was a sober depiction of fallen human nature. But there was grace. And in this story, we discovered grace in the presence of the peacock. From the introduction of the peacock, where we see its attention "fixed in the distance on something no one else could see," his occasional appearances in the story bring mystery and some sense of redemption from the disfunction around him.

Standing alone in the front yard, I appeared to be the only witness to this stunning peacock appearance. I watched quietly and in awe as he moved at a slow, determined pace across what had recently been a brome field. His iridescent blue neck shone in the sun, and the bright green tail feathers dotted with eyespots trailed behind him. The tuft of feathers on his head bobbed with each step. This peacock walked with a mild demeanor, not fearful, not flamboyant. While he made his way across the yard, I was transfixed. But, by the time he reached the road, I came to life.

I want him!!! I can't let him get away! I thought.

I was on a mission. At that moment, five-year-old Caleb and two-and-a-half-year-old Joshua came bouncing around the side of the house. "Hey, boys, let's go find that peacock," I shouted to them. Always ready for adventure, they gladly joined my quest. Grabbing Josh's hand, I pulled him toward the road. Caleb followed at a trot.

The peacock had disappeared into the cedar forest by the time the boys and I started searching, but I was sure we could find him. I began rationalizing how and why I could capture and claim this peacock, my peacock, my little Christ figure.

He hadn't seemed to be in a hurry. Of course, I tried to convince myself, he is tame. He has to be if he walked across the yard so close to me. In all probability, he is waiting to be captured and owned.

And I wanted to be the one to capture him and own him! Then I would forever have my confirmation that this move was a blessed decision.

The boys and I made our way down the road while my eyes scoured the bank, trying to find his path up into the woods. I could faintly remember the call of a peacock, and I managed a few weak sounds: *Eee-e-yoy eee-e-yoy, Eee-e-yoy eee-e-yoy!*

We were ready to go up the bank into the woods when Caleb said in a persuasive tone, "No, Oma! I saw the peacock go that way," as he pointed back the way we had just come. I was so determined to find this peacock that I suspended all reason ... and I followed the advice of a just-turned-five little boy. By the time we got back to where we had started, Caleb turned to me, grinning. "This is just a game, isn't it, Oma?"

My heart sank into my dusty shoes. By now, my peacock friend would be far into the woods. "No, Caleb, I did see a peacock. It wasn't a game," I murmured defeatedly. He would never understand what had just happened. Hesitatingly, I continued, "But ... that's okay. Maybe someday he will come back again."

Ah, the folly of thinking one can capture and forever hold those fleeting moments of "seeing" that God allows in our lives. And the greed! I wanted to grasp in my hand God's gift and hold it so I could prove to myself over and over God's blessing on our new home.

In the years that have followed, this home has now seen its own "heap of livin'." Many, many old friends and new friends have graced its interior. We have listened to heartaches, discussed profound ideas, and prayed with others for wisdom and understanding while seated around the table or in comfortable chairs in the den. Shouts of grandchildren, banging screen doors, cookie crumbs on the floor, handprints on the windows are becoming part of its history and blessed memories.

And across the road, life continues as it had. We can join into all that is going on, or we can sit back and appreciate the continuing ministry that the farm holds out to all who step through its gates.

I move gratefully forward now, knowing that the God who can send peacocks can continue to infuse our everyday lives with his undying grace ... always and wherever.

Since that moving day, rumors have surfaced of a lone peacock who made his home with a family a mile down Kitten Creek Road.

PRAYER MEETING WITH THE COWS

by Nancy Swihart

I skipped down the worn path to the old dairy barn where Daddy and our hired man, Shermy, were doing the evening milking chores. The barn was a magnet for my four-year-old soul. I loved the whole scene: the soft glow from the old ceiling lights, the lowing of cattle, the scent of fresh hay, and the very essence of what farming with animals is all about.

Born in Center County, Pennsylvania, I was four years old when my family bought a dairy farm set in the rocky, hilly soil of New York State. Although the scene was humble, my life was magical on that farm. Fields to roam, barns to explore, and the tightly structured life of dairy farming all fit together into a cocoon of beauty and pleasure for me.

And then there were the animals: chickens, ducks, horses, cats, and a new puppy. And, of course, the main characters, the dairy cows. Nothing is more charming to me than the gentle, expressive eyes of a cow. We somehow communicated when those cow eyes gazed into mine.

At four, I discovered how to get a barn full of those beautiful eyes to focus on my tiny inconspicuous frame.

I had invented a plan. After the ladies had been milked and were still in their stanchions nibbling on hay, I would wait patiently for Daddy and Shermy to leave to wherever their next job took them. I wanted to be the only human in the milking barn.

As soon as the barn was empty of other humans, I became the person in charge.

Grabbing an old scoop from an open feed sack by the back steps, I filled it with sweet grain, which was candy to the cows. My audience watched eagerly as the grain dribbled from my scoop into each of their troughs.

Soon all those beautiful eyes were carefully watching me. I had captured a grand audience.

What next? According to my limited experience, this would be easy: when lots of bodies gather together informally, you usually have a birthday party or a prayer meeting! At least, that was the extent of my four-year-old experiences.

Since we had had a birthday party for Bumpy the last time the cows and I had informally met, I opted for a prayer meeting this evening. But I needed a sermon.

Digging into my repertoire of learned homilies, I came up with what I thought would be appropriate.

"Ladies, Jesus loves you, and he died for your sins," I explained in my loud preacherly voice. A row of innocent eyes peered back. I figured they probably already knew that, but a reminder is always in good order.

"Okay." Seeing no response, I went on to the next plan. "Are there any prayer requests?"

Again, no response.

I could see that I was losing Bertha and Daisy, who were getting ready to lie down for the evening. Going back to the grain sack, I managed to scoop out another little dessert for my apathetic congregation. Maybe a birthday party would have been a better idea!

I don't know how many evenings I spent having birthday parties and prayer meetings with my bovine friends, but I do remember the last time.

My little soirees in the barn came to a close the evening I had a surprise intruder.

I think we had just started the prayer time when, from somewhere in the middle of the barn, came a loud, *Moo*.

Startled, I stopped and looked around. I was not used to being interrupted.

"Who said that?" I shouted accusingly, looking down the line of unbowed heads. Nobody stepped forward. So, I asked again in my most adult-like voice, "Who said that?"

From the bowels of the darkest part of the barn, I heard another "Mooooo." And then, laughter. Daddy, in his old overalls, stepped out of the shadows.

If a four-year-old can be embarrassed down to the tips of her toes, that was this little girl. I had been caught! Now my secret was out.

I was done.

Walking hand-in-hand with my daddy, back up the path to the house where dinner was waiting, I realized something had changed. The barn had become just a barn again with cows that needed to be milked. Yet, magic would always be waiting when my young imagination took hold once more.

Of course, my little escapade became a family story for years, with laughter and with a knowing look that this is just the way Nancy is.

Seventy-some years later, I fondly remember my little "prayer meetings" with the cows. I still talk to animals as though they understand me; and most of the time, I pretty much understand them.

I no longer get embarrassed when someone catches me rolling down the window and "mooing" to a cow who is standing forlornly in a field by the side of the road. Even my husband, Judd, who does not talk to animals or know what they say, has finally become resigned to the conversations I have with my animals, acknowledging, "This is just who Nancy is."

A COUNTRY PASTOR-FARMER'S FLOCK

by Dennis Ellingson

While I was serving as a pastor to a little country church in the high desert farm country of Southern Oregon, I read Philip Keller's wonderful book, *A Shepherd Looks at Psalm 23* and got interested in raising sheep.

About that time we were keeping two pregnant ewes for our friends Jon and Connie, and the ewes gave birth to female lambs.

Then a friend offered us a beautiful, 300-pound black ram named Bubba. He was huge and very tame. A sweet fellow, he had grown up as a bottle baby. Children could ride him. And he loved attention. So much so that whenever we sat down in the barnyard, he tried to sit on our laps! Imagine a 300-pound sheep sitting on you!

We had Bubba for a long time, and he provided us many lambs.

We also had a goat named Billy Bob who was quite rambunctious and mischievous. If you have ever had goats, you know one goat is one too many. He and Bubba stayed in the same area, but now and then they would both get out and head to my garden—usually while I was away. When I returned, Billy Bob would prance around and be hard to catch. But old Bubba would hang his head and head right back to his area. He seemed to feel quite guilty.

Eventually, when we moved to town, we returned Bubba

to our friend Gus. Gus said he would be working and feel a bump to his legs. This was Bubba wanting attention. Eventually his black coat turned white. We miss the sweet fellow to this day.

I would often use our interactions with sheep as sermon illustrations. For instance, we learned that shepherds don't lead from the front but from behind. We purposely did not have a sheep dog. We wanted to do the herding work ourselves. Yes, it was work; but even more, it was fun. Our first two ewes gave us two more ewes. Our grandson named them Twinkle-Twinkle and Little Star. He was a small boy at the time and loved coming out to the farm. And, yes, we did raise sheep for meat; but we could never use our own. We bought meat from a neighbor.

As Twinkle-Twinkle and Star grew up, Twinkle became quite fat, and so her name changed to "Twinkie." Star kept her original name, as she was distant and never seemed to feel comfortable with us. Twinkie was a sweetheart like Bubba and loved attention. She, like Bubba, wanted to be in our laps but was usually content to lie next to us. Our work at that time was fulfilling but quite stressful. Often, at the end of the day, we would spend time with the sheep just to relax. They gave us a sense of peace, and it seemed to be mutual. Star, though, would keep her distance, only occasionally lying nearby us.

When we had the sheep sheared in the summer, most of the sheep were fine with coming out and getting the yearly hair cut. But Star was another story. She beat me up good once as I tried wrestling her out of the shed, leaving me bloodied and bruised. But finally she seemed to figure out I was just trying to help.

A little time went by, and one cool evening we were

assisting Twinkie in birthing some babies down in the field, with sheep gathered around. But this time was different. Star came up to me, nuzzled a bit and then flopped down next to me and from then on she was very comfortable with me.

Perhaps the lesson is trust. Coming to trust in the Lord takes a while for some of us, too.

A Hedgehog like Bobo
(p. 152)

Dostoevsky the Iguana with some of Judy
Pex's grandchildren and friends
(p. 162)

A Cricket like Carol O'Casey's
childhood pet (p. 147)
and those of the Chinese (p. 152)

OUR UNUSUAL PETS

"Animals are footprints of God."

–Martin Luther

"Everything began to make sense—not just my relationship to God, but to the pelicans and the tree frogs and bees."

–Patricia Adams Farmer

GRACE SINGS ON CRICKET WINGS

by Carol O'Casey

Normal kids have a dog, cat, or perhaps a fish for a pet. I was not normal. My pet had an exoskeleton. My pet wore its ears on its knees. And my pet lived in a bamboo pagoda. At least his name was normal. Cricket was a cricket.

Bought on the streets of Chinatown in Los Angeles circa 1970, I carried him home to the suburbs of Orange County where he spent long nights calling to the crickets just beyond the screen of my bedroom window. I can still remember lying in bed, transfixed by his pure and simple song. Many a summer night of my childhood, the unmerited favor of the cricket song lulled me to sleep.

Crickets have captivated our species with their song for two-thousand years. Cricket keeping began in the Tang Dynasty (618-906 A.D.) as a pastime of aristocrats and emperor's concubines. Eventually the cricket-collecting custom spread to the common peoples of China and became an honored Chinese tradition.

While I spent hours watching my fenced fiddler perform, effortlessly rubbing his wings together, it wasn't till years later in a college entomology class that I actually learned how the cricket produces its characteristic chirp. Remember the childhood trick of playing the comb with your fingernail? The process is quite similar. Each wing of a male cricket is designed with a large, toothed, ridge-like vein underneath, topped with a file-like scraper. Raising his wings at a forty-five degree angle, he prepares to perform, drawing the ridge-like teeth (think comb) beneath one wing against the scraper (think nail) on the upper edge of the other wing. Female crickets lack these defined, sound-producing structures on their wings. They do, however, have ears to hear. Ingeniously tucked just below their kneecaps, these ears (small oval discs, much like the eye of a needle) allow them to tune in to their suitors' songs. How cool is that?

Following the cricket-collecting stage of my adolescence, I eventually emerged into the safe and sound stage of adulthood. Much as my cricket in the cage, I sang the song of sameness. Ordinary days follow predictable nights. Life was good but routine. For seventeen years, my husband and I pastored a church. Much of my identity was tied to that church. I had become the classic PW (pronounced "P-Dub," that great moniker bestowed on all pastor's wives)—a good wife, multi-tasking mother, and weekly Bible study leader. My life consisted of a heavy dose of church with a touch of my passion—field biology—sprinkled on the side. I kept these spheres neatly divided, separated by my erroneous belief that church and biology didn't mix.

During those years I kept God much as I kept my pet cricket—caged, and safely ensconced in my routine, my demands, and my comfort zone. He performed on my schedule; his song was solely for my enjoyment. I saw to it that I fed my God regularly with church attendance and all things religious. I tossed him tasty morsels of deeds done in his name. I liked my God in the cage. This way, I controlled my life. Were I to free him from the cage, I risked a life turned upside down, changed and unknown.

My life became fenced within my fears. My comfort zone defined a happy little enclosure all about me. I was secure. Secure in my relationships. Secure in my job. Secure in my church.... Security and sameness swallowed my soul.

My life resembled a walnut, neatly compartmentalized and tucked in a smooth, round shell. And God, being God, let me have my way for a time. But he was about to teach me a lesson, in a shell-breaking, cage-busting, unscheduled, and very non-routine way.

Before we go there, it is crucial to know what happened to my caged cricket. Eventually, after days of feeding Cricket lettuce, bran and watermelon slices, a delectable feast to be sure, I began to wrestle with reason. On the one hand, I enjoyed my pet dutifully serenading me to sleep each night. On the other, it pained me to see him caged in an artificial life of sameness. Although he voraciously chomped on melon, much of the day he lay listless. My conscience gnawed at my mind. The thought that Cricket may die in his bamboo prison terrified me.

One night, as the crickets in the distance called to him, I pushed the screen off my window and released Cricket into his element, free to be. I imagined him scurrying over the fresh garden soil, his legs brushing against the carrot tops as he raced to his kind. With the chorus of crickets drumming in my ears, I knew I heard Cricket singing his pure and clear song of freedom.

It would be thirty years before I would hear that grace-filled song again. And when I did, it came not on cricket wings, but on the wings of God.... In 2006, my husband received three unsolicited job offers in a period of nine months. A sense of impending doom hung heavy on my heart as I saw change hovering just above the horizon. Confronted with three of my deepest fears—change, risk, and the unknown—I entered a phase of resistance. I did not want to move. Period. My resistance prevailed, and my husband politely refused the first two offers. However, as often is the case when God has a plan, the third job offer appeared. Worn down by God's persistence, I acquiesced and my husband accepted the challenge to revive a struggling, dying church in a rural community. This job, incidentally, made the first two job offers look like a day at the beach. With the faith of a flea, I struggled to grasp any thread of hope to carry me through. I knew in my heart that God had my back, but my brain strained to catch up with my heart.

During this year of turmoil, I learned to listen to the Master. Little did I know he was preparing to give me a new song. What needed to happen was a blending of tones, a symphonic merger, if you will.

Like that fiddler cricket making beautiful music with two structurally different wings, I needed to unite the wing of my biologist "bow" with the "string" of my Christianity. United wings are harmonic wings. Just one problem: I was out of practice. No, that's not entirely true. I had never practiced. I kept my "wings" in pristine condition, silent and separate.

Catholic priest and author Thomas Berry, in his book *The Great Work*, eloquently explained the mechanics of merging nature with spirituality:

> *The outer world is necessary for the inner world; they are not two worlds, but a single world with two aspects.... We need the sun, the moon, the stars, the rivers and the mountains and birds, the fish in the sea, to evoke a world of mystery, to evoke the sacred. It gives us a sense of awe.*

I believed this. I knew firsthand the benefits of uniting the outer world of nature with the inner world of the soul. Yet I remained silent on sharing the power of God in nature. Perhaps I needed rosin, the human fiddler's friend. Let me explain. Rosin, a natural component of tree sap, allows the bow to grip the strings of the instrument and is responsible for producing full resonating sound. No rosin? Then no grip, no sound. I needed spiritual rosin to allow my "string"and "bow" to resonate with a new, beautiful song that sang of the wonders of creation.

The move to central Oregon only magnified my need to refine my purpose. I left behind my job and close friends. I wrestled with purpose for months. Then on a crisp fall day in 2007, I hiked to a knoll overlooking the Big Deschutes River. Leaning back against an ancient, gnarled Ponderosa pine I prayed,

> *Okay, God, here I am. Show me how to unite the spheres of my life. Give me purpose. Help me glorify you with my passion for creation.*

And my faithful Father answered his lost and lonely child. Deep in my soul I received refreshing raindrops of grace—the rosin I needed.

The Greek word for grace is *charis*, which literally means "that which affords joy, pleasure, delight, sweetness, charm, loveliness." With great pleasure, and much joy, I finally felt free to pursue the person God created me to be—the wildlife loving, wilderness wandering me—instead of who I thought I was expected to be. This didn't happen overnight. And it certainly wasn't easy. Slowly, one small step at a time, God led me forward on this journey.

God infuses the symphony of our lives with grace notes: we have the freedom to choose the melody that makes our lives sing. We are not to play a life score written by someone else. We are free to dance to the beat of our own heart, guided by the conductor of life himself.

BO BO, THE HEDGEHOG

by Susan Elaine Jenkins

When I first moved across the Pacific Ocean to settle into expatriate life in northern China, it soon became apparent that there were no pets, other than crickets and birds carried in cages to parks by older men. There, the wooden cages—some quite elaborately carved—were hung on branches of Scholar or Red Ash trees, while their owners spent a few hours drinking tea, smoking cigarettes, and playing friendly games of shuffleboard or ping pong. The familiar clicking sound of mahjong tiles mingled with the chatter of birds as groups of four huddled around flimsy cardboard tables. Then, as the shadows began to fall across the grounds, the men proudly carried their pets back to their crumbling brick hutongs for the night.

It had only been a few weeks, but I could sense the absence of cats and dogs, probably because I had grown up in a home where dogs were part of the family. Their personalities were great sources of joy for us, as they wagged, played, and loved us as only a dog can do. The void in this northern city of 59-million people was almost palpable, and I asked my neighbor Ouyang about it one night as we sat at his mother's gleaming rosewood table.

As I fished out morsels of chicken with my chopsticks, I asked, "No one has pet dogs here, do they?"

Ouyang narrowed his eyes and shook his head, "Of

course not, no. Cats and dogs are considered to be food, Susan. People would feel shame to raise one in their homes when so many do not have enough to eat."

As we talked quietly, the sun began to set. Ouyang's mother delivered a succession of small platters bearing expertly prepared food—hot peanuts sizzling in ginger sauce, sauteed celery with fried tofu slices or shrimp dumplings dipped in aromatic sauce. As we ate, Ouyang told me stories of growing up in the 1960s, during the height of the Cultural Revolution, when his mother had to make a single bowl of rice last for three days. He explained that, while the current situation was better, the memories were sharp and painful. People were only just now beginning to have enough to eat. For many Chinese people, these days were the first in decades that one's appetite could be satiated. Now, children could eat all they wanted—crisp apples, glistening chunks of beef, or hard-boiled eggs to assist their brains as they studied. Ouyang explained that while he felt it was wrong to consume meat from animals such as dogs and cats, many people had to choose between that and starvation just three decades earlier.

One day, while meandering around the streets surrounding my school and home, I noticed a storefront that boasted an over sized photograph of a cute, white puppy. Thinking it was a pet store, and that a dog would be a welcome addition to my home, I entered, and was surprised to find that it was a dog restaurant. Dog soup, dog with mushrooms, or dog with tomatoes. Not what I was expecting—I was astonished and sickened.

One evening we were dining at another of the many small restaurants that dotted our neighborhood streets, and Ouyang told me about the day in his childhood, when at the age of eight, with one pigtail jetting off the side of his head, he wandered through a garden gate that had been left ajar for a moment, curious and compelled by the beauty of the roses.

A kindly older gentleman, Mr. Dao, noticed the small lad, watched him bury his face into the velvety blooms, and had decided to invite him to come back the following afternoon. Ouyang was eager to spend time there, and soon he was stopping every day to visit with Uncle Dao, who shared his wisdom and love for gardening with the little boy. The two became inseparable. He enjoyed a freedom that he didn't have when he was at home—as the constant fear of being called out by the violent Red Guards controlled many aspects of life in his home. When Ouyang practiced the violin, his mother had to shut all the windows—the enjoyment of music was something for which one could be harshly punished, or even killed. People were physically tormented for reading books, playing the piano, wearing colorful clothing, or having long hair. The pursuit of pleasure was strictly prohibited, even gardening, unless it was a government-sanctioned garden, such as Mr. Dao's. Ouyang's daily visits to the lush garden became a trigger of joy for him—a chance to share beauty with the gentle keeper of the garden that he soon called Uncle Dao, out of reverential respect.

One day, as he quietly unlatched the iron gate and entered the maze of rose bushes, he was met by Mr. Dao, whose eyes disappeared in a face that resembled a wrinkled walnut, when he smiled. He put his finger to his lips. "Shhh...be very quiet. I have something special for you today, Little Ouyang."

Ouyang stood still while his friend disappeared into the small room, then he emerged with a little hedgehog in his hands. Little Ouyang's eyes grew big in surprise, and he immediately reached out to gingerly touch the spiky body.

"May I touch it?"

Mr. Dao nodded slowly, and showed the little boy how to hold it safely in his trembling hands. "You see how the spikes are evenly distributed, which makes it possible to hold it, yes?"

Ouyang nodded and asked, "Where did you find it, Uncle Dao?"

"I saw something floating in the small river behind the back gates, and I was curious. I thought it was a dead animal, but when I reached out for it, I realized it was still alive. I was surprised to find it was a hedgehog! Such a mysterious and strange thing to find in the river, yes? So I brought it home for a while."

Little Ouyang couldn't take his eyes off the little hedgehog. "Uncle Dao, I've always wanted a pet! My father brought home a book from Canada about a boy with a puppy, but Mama and Baba* say that is impossible. And now I can have a hedgehog for a pet, yes?"

Mr. Dao nodded cautiously, "Yes, you can have this hedgehog as a pet, but for only a little while. He will grow to be too big, perhaps, and then we will let it go free. But for a while he can be your pet. What would you like to name him, Little Ouyang?"

"Bo Bo! I would like to call him Bo Bo!"

Mr. Dao nodded in approval. "That is a perfect name for him. He looks like a Bo Bo, doesn't he?"

"Yes! He is so cute. His nose is long and his eyes look like black buttons!"

Little Ouyang carefully held him for a few more moments, then he regretfully said, "I have to go home now, before it gets dark. Can I take it home with me? I want to show Mama and Baba!"

Mr. Dao shook his head, "I don't think that would be wise, Little Ouyang. So many these days are looking out

---

* Chinese for "Papa"

for any who break the rules, who step out with new ideas. A pet hedgehog might raise suspicions about your family, and—well, in the times we're living in, that would be ample cause for one of your parents to be sent to feed pigs in the countryside. We don't want that to happen. No, I think I will keep the hedgehog right here with me, and you can come to visit every day. He'll be your pet, of course. But I will watch over him."

Ouyang held and tried to cuddle the hedgehog the best he could. He thought Bo Bo might enjoy hearing one of the songs he had learned in school, so he softly sang, with Mr. Dao reminding him to sing very quietly.

Hello, hello, my friend
How are you today?
I am your good friend
You are my good friend
Good-bye, my friend!

The next afternoon, he bounded into the garden, anxious to hold his new pet. He discovered that Mr. Dao had been able to borrow a large cage from one of his friends. Little Ouyang thought that Bo Bo loved his new home.

"Thank you for the cage, Uncle Dao!"

Mr. Dao's smile disappeared. "I am enjoying having Bo Bo here with me, Little Ouyang, but the day is soon coming when you will need to let him go live his natural life. I cannot provide the kind of food he needs, and I also am afraid the Red Guards will discover that he is living here. Pets, other than birds and crickets, are strictly forbidden."

Sadly, after a few weeks, the hedgehog had grown to such a size, Mr. Dao decided it needed to go free. He managed to explain this to the eight year old Ouyang, and together they carried the cage to an area with grassland.

Tears fell from his eyes as they placed Bo Bo onto the ground and watched him take off across the meadow. Mr. Dao, his loyal friend, stood beside him, with one arm wrapped lovingly around the little boy. Little Ouyang sang softly,

Hello, hello, my friend
How are you today?
I am your good friend
You are my good friend
Good-bye, my friend!

When I met Ouyang, he was thirty-eight years of age, but could remember his days with Bo Bo, the hedgehog as if they were yesterday.

"When Bo Bo became my pet hedgehog, there was only darkness all around me. The streets were dangerous places and the fear reached into every part of my life and even into my home. But for those weeks, a lighter place developed—a place where the sadness and darkness could not reach. The love I felt for Bo Bo and Uncle Dao was in stark contrast to the sadness of life outside the gate."

Ouyang was my neighbor for three remarkable years, and it was a sad day when I had to say good-bye to him and his mother, as I moved to the southern city of Guangzhou. During my seven years there, a few dogs gradually joined the throngs of people who spent time outdoors, as the Chinese people do. And then, five years later, I was living on the eastern seaboard of China in the wonderful city of Ningbo, where it became common to see fluffy white dogs being walked by their proud owners early in the mornings and then again as the sun dropped over the small lake that stretched behind the neighborhood.

The day when people could no longer have pet dogs and

cats had come to a happy end, and I could hear their barking and watch them frolic on the many walking pathways that meandered through the maze of high-rises where I lived. It was a joy to see so many dogs being lovingly raised as full-fledged members of the Chinese families. The atmosphere was pleasant, as neighbors walked the dogs in their pajamas, cordially greeting their neighbors and wishing them a good day, while smiling proudly at their pets.

Ouyang continues to look back on his happy afternoons with Mr. Dao and Bo Bo the hedgehog with great joy. He has never acquired another animal, as he keeps very busy with travel for his flourishing export business; but his small, spiky hedgehog with the bright black eyes will always have a treasured place in his heart.

TOADS AND SALAMANDERS

by Catherine Lawton

I have found that spiritual, emotional, and physical healing can begin even in times that are darkened, cold, alone, silent ... when I still my heart and contemplate the "treasures of darkness" (Isaiah 45:3). One of the sweetest treasures of darkness is the realization that we are not alone. That realization encouraged me anew this past winter as I considered how nature also experiences waiting, something that has become more acute for us during a pandemic.

In much of the Northern Hemisphere, at least, we wait during winter for lighter, warmer days of nature's renewal. And during the days of Lent we recall Jesus' crucified body waiting in a dark, cold cave of death.

I asked myself, "When Jesus 'woke up' in that cave of a tomb, did he open his eyes to darkness? Or did his open eyes, his very breath and resurrection-life energy, shine light into the darkness even before the stone rolled away?" John wrote that Jesus is the light and the light shines in the darkness and the darkness has not overcome it (John 1:5).

We can experience moments during periods of waiting that are holy, even healing. One winter morning during the Covid-19 pandemic I sat in meditative prayer in a corner room of our basement. That room has two windows with below-ground-level window wells.

During the summer, toads and tiger salamanders dwell in the window wells. My grandchildren like to look for them. During winter, these denizens of the deep dig into the earth and wait in darkness, finally emerging again in mid spring when the ground thaws and days lengthen and the sun travels higher and warmer and farther across the sky.

When Cottontail Rabbit babies fall into the window wells, we rescue and release them into the tall, natural grasses nearby. One summer a Green Razorback Snake resided in one well. The Spadefoot Toads and Tiger Salamanders are signs of the warming of spring, when all that has been dormant, hibernating, or buried break through, come out, breathing and hungry, stretching and growing and reaching toward light and life and love.

Toads and Salamanders aren't high on the food chain or evolutionary heirarchy, but I treasure the lessons they teach me with their watchful, beady eyes, hopefulness in looking up toward the heights for bugs and raindrops to fall, their responsiveness to light and motion and moisture and warmth. And how their seeming resurrection reminds me that Jesus went down into darkness and death for us and came back up and out, alive. Some day we and the loved ones whose bodies or ashes we have buried will be resurrected to everlasting spring.

On that cold, sequestered pandemic morning, as I considered these creatures—and my own sense of waiting—this poem came to me:

HOLY STILLNESS

There is no heartbeat
in a seed
Yet life waits
in that brittle encasement
as surely as in the stilled
breathing and slowed
beating heart of
toads and salamanders
in winter deeps and
sleeping bears in caves

Waiting, waiting, we wait
in lengthened nights and
chilled soil and cloistered suns
for warmer, lighter, moister days
to dawn
From on high—and pulsing
in the depths—we hear
"Wait... Wait... Be still..."
and "Coming—
I did, I am, I will."

DOSTOEVSKY THE IGUANA

by Judith Galblum Pex

S ometimes, what seems to be good or positive, through the perspective of time later proves to be not what it seemed, although this doesn't negate the original experience. A job or a relationship that started well and brought fruit might not work out long term. Yet I believe God wants to use everything for our good, and we will learn lessons if we look for them.

Sitting around the dinner table one evening, our fifteen-year-old daughter, Racheli, surprised us with an idea for a new pet.

"I'd like an iguana for my birthday next week," she said.

"Why an iguana?" my husband, John, asked. "Aren't Peewee and Nala enough pets for us?"

"Iguanas are cool," she said.

"Sure," I said. "They're cold-blooded animals, not cute and fuzzy, but what do they actually do? It won't follow you around or learn tricks like Peewee, or purr and sit on your lap like Nala."

"They're green," she said. "And they look like dragons."

"Do they even sell them in Eilat?" John asked. Eilat, where we live, is a small town in the south of Israel, five hours from Tel Aviv and four from Jerusalem with limited shopping options.

"Moriah and I already went to the pet store," Racheli said. She exchanged looks with our younger daughter.

"It was cute," cracked Moriah with a smile. "It's Green. And this big." She spread her hands apart.

"Abba and I'll think about it," I said. "Where would it live?"

"That aquarium left over from the fish that died would probably work...." said John. When he began thinking aloud like this, I knew he'd made up his mind.

Life with four teenagers was never boring. Raising our children in a third culture, Israel, other than the ones John and I grew up in, the United States and Holland, and being followers of Jesus (a tiny minority here) added to our challenges. Like most parents, we sought ways to affirm our children, strengthen our family structure, and minimize arguments, saving them for things we felt were important. We'd already decided that music, hair, and clothing styles weren't issues, so maybe a pet lizard would also help Racheli express her individuality, something all teenagers need.

"Pets are good for teaching responsibility," I said to John.

"Can't think of any reason not to agree," he said.

We didn't know at the time that iguanas grow to be huge—two meters in length and weighing ten kilos, they need a large enclosure (some people suggest giving iguanas their own small room), they have a lifespan of up to twenty years, and they are incredibly strong.

The children outfitted the aquarium with newspapers on the bottom, a large water bowl, and branches and rocks for climbing. Also importantly, as the man in the pet store told us, we needed a seventy-five watt light bulb for basking and heating. Looking back, I'm amazed how little we knew about iguana care. In those days before googling, we didn't have access to information as we do today and simply expected things to work out.

The big day arrived, Racheli's birthday and our iguana's

adoption. As she gently placed him in his cage, the six of us stood in front of it and gazed on him with admiration.

"He looks happy," Racheli said.

"Hope so," I said. "But what makes you say that?"

"He's glad to leave the pet store," she said. "And look, he's eating the lettuce."

"What's his name?" John asked.

"Dostoevsky."

"You're kidding," I said.

"No, that's it." Dostoevsky the iguana.

Iguanas as pets obviously weren't unknown in Israel, since the pet store in our small town sold them. But they were rare.

Dostoevsky became a sensation among our children's friends. A stream of teenagers came by our house after school to view our emerald-green lizard.

"Gives me a chance to put faces to the names I've been hearing from the kids," I said to John. I'd always liked the idea of our house being a hangout rather than our children going elsewhere.

Racheli and the other children picked up and held Dostoevsky every day, wanting to help him adjust to human contact. In the beginning, he kept both eyes closed when being held but slowly began opening one of them.

"At first he was trying to shut us out," Racheli said. "But now with his eye open, he feels more relaxed and willing to interact with people." Our sensitive daughter quickly understood people's feelings and also iguana's, it seemed.

She often sat or walked around the house with the iguana on her shoulder. "He likes the view from up here," she said, "because iguanas climb trees in the wild."

Dostoevsky's climbing also led him to rest on the back of our sofa where he could lie still for hours. Before we warned them, an unsuspecting guests in our home might take a comfortable seat, lean back, and suddenly discover their headrest was a live iguana.

Again, with no internet search engine or Wikipedia in those days, our interpretation of Dosty's (his nickname) behavior was speculation. Though we weren't bonding with him as with a dog or cat, he was becoming a familiar feature in our home. When we came in the front door, the first thing all of us did was to glance at Dosty's cage.

He wasn't always there, however, because we began allowing him to wander around the house which in his own way, he seemed to appreciate. How could we tell he was happy when he didn't wag his tail or cuddle on our laps? Well, every time he was set free, we would find him in a different spot so he obviously liked exploring.

We had to remember to shut our front door. Living in a warm climate and small town, we kept it wide open most of the day.

"Where's Dostoevsky?" became a familiar saying in our home.

He could easily climb the carpeted stairs to our second floor and seemed to like hiding himself in small places.

We would then join forces as a family to seek our wayward, curious iguana.

"He could be anywhere," Racheli said on one occasion. "I hope the door was closed."

"He likes it under the sofa," I said. "But he isn't there this time. Each one should carefully check their own room."

"Found him!" Moriah called, and we all rushed upstairs to see Dosty lying behind a pile of clothes in her wardrobe oblivious to the worry he'd created.

"Let's try to keep all doors closed from now on," I said. "Front door, bedrooms, and also wardrobes. That will make life simpler."

When Dostoevsky grew out of his original aquarium,

we acquired a larger one which held a prominent place in our living room for years. He was already a meter long, including his tail, and the children were also growing up. Only two were still teenagers.

Returning from a trip abroad, John and I and our two youngest children stepped out of the car, and Joshua met us in the front yard, fidgeting with his hands and looking down at the ground.

He spoke softly. "I'm sorry…it's Dosty."

My chest tightened. Surely nothing serious could have happened to our pet?

"Two days ago, he looked apathetic and wasn't moving, and when I picked him up, I noticed a small scratch on his front leg with a tiny spot of blood."

Yonatan rubbed his hand across his head and Moriah's chin trembled.

Josh spoke in a monotone. "Maybe I should have noticed his suffering sooner. I took him to the vet who said there wasn't much to do but gave him a shot of adrenaline anyway. He probably cut himself on one of his adventures or on a sharp edge of the aquarium."

I threw my arms around Josh and brushed a tear from my eye, in pain for Dosty but also for Josh. "It's not your fault."

"My friend helped me bury him in the desert."

John removed Dostoevsky's aquarium from our living room and in its space I set a large house plant, but his place in our hearts took longer to fill. I had never imagined our family becoming so attached to a cold-blooded lizard and the sadness his passing would cause. I should have known, though, because each time we love or connect with someone, we become vulnerable and set ourselves up for pain with their parting.

I learned that even a scaly creature can engender empathy, and after living with Dosty for years, we could read his body language in his posture, dewlap, swagger, and head bobbing. I missed our family's hide-and-seek games and the thrill of finding Dosty. I missed family and friends from far and wide coming and wanting to touch or hold our exotic, photogenic pet.

Our four children are grown now and have blessed us with nine grandchildren. Looking back, we have mixed feelings as we remember the time Dostoevsky lived with us.

"It's not right to keep an iguana," Moriah said recently. "They're not like cats and dogs that are bred to live with people."

"That's a modern concept," I said. "When we took him, people didn't think like that."

Am I sorry we adopted an iguana? No, in those critical years with four teenagers at home, Dosty filled a special place in our family. He was a magnet and our mascot.

Would I recommend for someone else to have a pet iguana? Not with what I know now, and I'm glad we didn't have to turn one of the children's bedrooms into a lizard's room!

HONEYBEES

by Catherine Lawton

My husband, Larry, and I had a beehive (sometimes two or three hives) in our backyard for a number of years.

Larry became an excellent beekeeper. The bees seemed to come to recognize and trust him. They didn't much like it when he opened their hive, but a little smoke calmed them. The protector bees would line up on the top edge of a hive frame, all facing Larry, ready to defend their queen, brood, and honey. But when he opened the hive, he always wore protective clothing and beekeeper's veil. Once he got "a bee in his bonnet." He felt the bee walking across his face but stayed calm (better than I would have done) while he walked away slowly from the hive and took off the veiled hat and released the bee.

We found out that honeybees are quite curious. We taught the grandchildren to stand a distance away to observe bees. Once a bee, flying back to the hive, laden with pollen from neighbors' flowers, flew by a little granddaughter and grazed against her cheek. She said, "The bee kissed me!"

Keeping bees gave us a vivid awareness of the interconnectedness of nature. Honeybees go out in a two-mile radius. The honey our bees produced varied in color depending on the season and from what flowers it was made: early spring dandelions along the roadsides, late spring flowers in people's gardens, mid summer alfalfa flowers in farm fields.

I planted many nectar-producing flowers for the bees.

When we welcomed bees into our gardens, the flowers, berries, and herbs flourished noticeably more. I was sure the salvia flower stalks and spearmint blossoms bloomed longer than they had before so many bees relished closeness with them. The flowers seemed to respond and love the honeybees as much as the bees delighted in the flowers and the nectar they produced. Of course we enjoyed seeing the well-being of our gardens and eating and sharing the honey that resulted!

The relationship I observed in my garden between the flowers and the bees reminded me of my prayer relationship with God. Listening to the honeybees buzzing and watching them busy on the flowers, I thought, *This must be a little like the way our relational God longs to commune with us, to create well-being within us, and to sweeten the course of the future with us, as we pray.* Deep calls to deep as God calls us to intimate prayer and contemplation. As we respond and allow the Spirit of God access, we can experience loving communion with Him. I believe that to be known by God in this open, mutual way is to be transformed.

It is much like the bees—both honeybees and wild bees—that seem to draw out more blooms and fruit from my garden. We can be looking for shalom to blossom and grow. Each one who truly cooperates in prayer and loving action with the Spirit of God increases God's kingdom, working for good and overcoming evil in this world.

"We know the whole creation has been groaning" (Romans 8:22), kind of like a garden longing to open its petals to sunshine and bees. Perhaps the world is waiting for us to respond to our almighty and ever-present God in open, obedient, watching-for-possibilities prayer. Perhaps the more people respond positively to the wooing of God, the more grace flows, like nectar flowing in an interconnected and well-pollinated garden.

Carol O'Casey (p. 147) hand feeding backyard birds

OUR WILD ANIMAL ENCOUNTERS

"Reflect upon the providence and wisdom of God in all created things and praise Him in them all."

–Teresa of Avila

"O Lord, how manifold are thy works! In wisdom hast thou made them all; the earth is full of thy creatures."

–Psalm 104:24

"He gives wild animals their food, including the young ravens when they cry...."

–Psalm 147:9

SWIMMING WITH DOLPHINS

by Judith Galblum Pex

Sometimes you need to escape your four walls and meet others, a common longing during the past Corona year. Here in Israel, I tried to comply with our three lockdowns and constantly changing and confusing restrictions as best I could when, most of the time, we weren't able to meet with more than ten people inside and at times were forbidden to travel more than a kilometer from home.

While I have much to be thankful for—no one close to me ill with Covid, a wonderful husband, and a new writing project prompted by the lockdown awakening my creative juices—yet with traveling and spending time with family eliminated, I needed an outlet. God provided one in an unexpected way, through dolphins.

Our town, Eilat, is the southernmost city in Israel, located on the Gulf of Eilat/Aqaba and is one of Israel's premier tourist spots, not for biblical sites like Jerusalem and the Galilee but for the clear blue sea, coral reefs, desert surroundings, and its many hotels, shops, and restaurants. We do, however, find mentions of Eilat in the Bible because Moses passed through here twice during the children of Israel's forty-year desert wanderings, and Solomon maintained a fleet of ships in Eilat. The Byzantines, Nabateans, Romans, and other peoples also had settlements on these shores.

After the first lockdown strictly closed down the entire country, our "virus czar" decided to allow individual sports.

"Eilat must be one of the best places to pass the Corona time," John said. "As long as we can go to the beach, we'll be fine." Since moving to Eilat from the U.S. forty-five years ago, except for a couple of the coldest winter months, we swim nearly every day finding it the perfect exercise for body, mind, and soul. I call it my moving meditation.

"Which beach today?" I asked when we were finally permitted to leave the house. Eilat has many beaches, each with its own character.

"Katza?" John said. "Maybe we'll see dolphins."

The Dolphin Reef, next to Katza beach and one of Eilat's popular attractions, was established to allow visitors to meet and observe dolphins in their natural habitat. It has no outer net, unlike other dolphin parks in the world; the dolphins are free to swim into the open sea, returning to the Reef because they enjoy interacting with the trainers and tourists and are fed there. Laid out with lush vegetation, beach chairs, shade, and a restaurant, guests can observe dolphins jumping and swimming. and for a higher fee than they've already paid to enter the site, can snorkel or dive with the dolphins.

We liked the Katza beach because, though it has no greenery, chairs, snack bar, or stunning coral reefs, there was no entrance payment, and we occasionally saw fins of dolphins in the distance or if we were lucky, one swam near us when it left the Reef.

For a city with a year-round tourism industry, on this day in May, Eilat felt like a ghost town as we drove on nearly empty roads, past the shut-down Dolphin Reef, and sat with a scattering of people on the beach.

Immediately upon arriving, John tossed his shirt and towel on the pebbly beach, put on his mask and snorkel, and dove into the water. I always take longer, savoring the views of the rugged Mountains of Edom opposite us and the still, turquoise waters which eventually join the Red Sea and from there flow into the Indian Ocean.

Twenty minutes later, John emerged from the sea, a grin creasing his face. "Two dolphins swam close to me," he said.

"I should have gone with you," I said. "But I'll give it a try, and maybe they'll still be around."

I swam in the direction of the Reef focusing on my breathing and on executing smooth freestyle strokes. Suddenly, from behind me, a large gray shape streamed by and then another. They were so close, I could look them in the eye, and they seemed to be gazing at me. I could have touched them but knew it's not allowed; all contact is meant to be from the dolphin's initiative.

As I saw their forms disappearing in the watery haze ahead of me, I began swimming after them with all my strength while knowing my efforts were useless; the dolphins are in their element and my movements a clumsy flailing in comparison. They turned around and this time passed under me, flipping over on their backs to reveal their white bellies. Like a dance or a game, they seemed to be enjoying themselves. And then they were gone, and I swam back to the beach. Stepping out of the sea, I removed my mask and grabbed a towel.

"You saw them too," John said, seeing my smile.

"Close-by, and they hung around with me for a while."

The following day, we went again to Katza beach and again, both of us met up with dolphins. We began heading there every day, looking forward to swimming with the dolphins and were rarely disappointed.

Sometimes we glimpsed a solitary one, sometimes all five who live at the Reef, sometimes they stayed around longer, and other times just zoomed by.

"Do you also hear their clicking sounds?" I asked John.

"Amazing," John said. "Though it's hard to know from which direction they're coming."

I knew dolphins are considered very intelligent mammals. When I researched more about them, I learned that those clicks, together with whistles, are their mode of communicating with each other, and each individual has its own unique "signature whistle." Just as astounding, through their echolocation—emitting sounds and listening to the echoes that return—dolphins are said to be able to detect the fetus in the womb of a pregnant woman.

The days we didn't meet dolphins showed me that they were seeking us out which made our encounters more special. I'd read that they're sociable creatures, and I could sense their curiosity. Their playfulness as they leapt out of the water, and smiles when they came up for air, reminded me of qualities I wanted to cultivate more in myself.

One afternoon, after a long swim without seeing dolphins, I came out of the sea and began drying off when I saw a fin break through the water's surface in the distance. Without a second thought, I donned my mask and snorkel, jumped in again, and began swimming quickly in the direction the fin had appeared. I soon found myself with a dolphin swimming in circles around and under me, mesmerizing me with its underwater acrobatics. I slowed down my speed, nearly coming to a halt, neither of us in a hurry to be anyplace else.

As I enjoyed those magical moments, time stopped until my feet and hands became numb from the cold. Reluctantly, because the dolphins had always left first, I parted from this streamlined, spirited creature and headed back to the shore. Swimming quickly, I suddenly felt a sharp bump on my forehead and found myself lifted into the air, startled but not hurt.

John met me with a towel. "I saw what happened," he said. "You shrieked and were tossed six feet in the air."

"I didn't know I shrieked," I said. "And I doubt it was six

feet, but that's the first time I've ever had a head bash from a dolphin. He didn't want me to go."

After a year, and thanks to an aggressive campaign in which over half Israel's population received Covid vaccinations within a few months, restrictions began to be lifted. We could venture further from our homes, tourists began returning to Eilat, and the Dolphin Reef reopened.

For the first few days following the end of the lockdown, we maintained our routine of going every afternoon to the Katza beach.

"Shall we give them a try again?" John suggested after four days in a row with no dolphin sightings.

"I can't bring myself to go there nowadays," I said, "hoping in vain a dolphin will swim by. They're not looking for us anymore."

John shook his head. "They can swim now with visitors to the Reef."

I miss the thrill of jumping in the water and not knowing how many dolphins I'll see and the wonder these beautiful creatures brought into my life. But whereas during the lockdowns, we sought the dolphins and they us, today we have other outlets and are able to gather freely again with our friends.

"Our time with the dolphins was unique," John said. "Let's go to Coral Beach now."

I agreed. "It was a privilege few people experience. And as long as Israel continues to succeed at fighting the virus, we may never have that opportunity again."

As we drove past Katza beach, I gazed over the calm sea knowing that dolphins were swimming around somewhere below the surface and remembered the lessons they taught me about playfulness, curiosity, savoring the moment, and the joy of being alive.

BACKYARD BIRDS

poems by Catherine Lawton

SPRINGTIME REUNIONS

Welcome back, friends, I'm bringing you seeds,
Birds in the bushes, birds in the trees.
Keep up the chattering, chirp and sing,
Birds on the grasses, birds on the breeze.

Display your colors, showcase your tune;
She'll hear, she'll see you—it won't be long—
Call from the housetop, she's perched at the gate,
Who could resist such a heartfelt song?

Birds playing games of "catch me if you can"
Soon build nests in Hawthorn and Cedar.
Eggs warm, babies fed, they grow up and remember;
Next spring to show up, back at my feeder.

BUSHTITS

Sprite, nimble on honeysuckle bushes:
   tiny, frisky, little flock
   hopping and feeding
   on sprigging branches—
   over, under, around, between,
Tink, tink, tinkling,
   like bells that ding
   no matter which way
   you turn them—
   even upside downing.
Buffy underneath
   gray wings,
   dark eyes in stunted faces,
   longish tails on
   puff-ball bodies.
Bringing ringing into my morning.

BEGINNER'S "LUCK"
My First Hunt

by Larry Lawton

A year after moving to Colorado I was invited to go elk hunting with newfound friends. They instructed me how to obtain an over-the-counter license for a specific hunting area. I didn't own a rifle and had no experience big game hunting, but I was excited to learn. I read brochures, watched instructional videos, and listened to my friends about hunting. One of these friends, Ray, took me under his wing and loaned me one of his rifles and a pair of woolen trousers, and suggested I purchase a good pair of insulated boots, warm jacket, required orange hat and vest, warm hunting gloves, and ammo. The license was good for the third season at the beginning of November, and it could be cold in the Rocky Mountains.

Ten of us assembled together near Gunnison, Colorado, close to Fossil Ridge at about 10,000 feet elevation, to set up camp. We would go out by twos in various directions. Most of the group had been hunting for over 35 years. We camped in relative luxury with a Dessert Storm Tent, two wood stoves (one with solid grill and oven), a table, indoor/outdoor carpeting, and room for ten cots.

On the first morning it began snowing as my partner, Greg, and I stood 75 feet off the side of a forest dirt road looking down into a small valley considered a 'bowl' with fairly thick forest of Aspen, Ponderosa Pine, Douglas Fir and Piñon Pines all around the ridge and thinning as they dropped the 100 yards to the meadow running through the middle of the valley below. One could see at various locations around the top of the ridge about a dozen spots of bright orange hats and vests.

As I looked down into the meadow on my right, all of a sudden there was a large bull elk running full speed, going left down through the middle of the bowl! It took me by surprise and I wasn't ready to fire my rifle. But multiple rifle shots sounded from around the top of the ridge as other hunters fired. The elk kept running as fast as he could and got away. I thought at the moment, how would one know if they were the one that actually hit the elk? It felt like a war zone to me.

Snow fell for the next two hours, as we trekked slowly and quietly up the road to find ourselves at the highest top of the ridge. Keeping near the edge of the trees we worked our way down near the middle of the valley to where the elk had exited the bowl and escaped the onslaught of bullets. I'm guessing this valley's meadow was a half mile long. We didn't see anything except hunters on the ridge so we made sure they acknowledged our orange by nodding at them.

Well, we didn't want the hunters above us shooting in our direction, so we finally made our way to the opposite lower end of the valley bottom to a narrow opening. There, a dirt road rounded to our left up the hill to where we first started our hunt. The road winds around because of the gain in elevation, and about half way up we noticed tracks in the snow crossing the road. Examining the size of the tracks, we determined they were elk and not deer. In the snow beside the road it wasn't clear which direction the animal had been walking. We started following what we thought was the right direction. Then, in the more grassy area, we saw that the tracks definitely went the opposite way across the road and down the slope. My partner with hunting experience walked ahead of me and I stayed about six feet behind as we followed the tracks.

We had only gone off the road down 50 feet through the Aspen grove when we spotted the elk. It was a bull and legal to shoot. It was close, about 50 feet away in the hundreds of Aspens. My partner aimed. But it was too close range for a clear view through the scope. He fired anyway, and missed.

The elk ran off to the right of us still about 50 feet away and stopped with his head in view just past an Aspen tree. I could not see the rest of his body because of the many trees. He turned his neck and head to look directly at me. My partner was safely on my left, which allowed me to shoot. I only had one clear opening between the trees and this elk was looking at me. Thinking the elk would soon run, with adrenalyn flowing, I aimed my rifle and waited for him to dart forward. I was ready.

But the elk quickly swung his head back the other way, turned his body, and retreated in the opposite direction, and vanished from our view. I didn't get to fire a shot.

The road we had left to track the elk actually swung around further up above us. As soon as the elk turned from my aim and ran for a few seconds across the Aspen forest we heard two shots rip through the trees coming from the road above. Scary!

Thinking I was so smart, with beginner's bravado, I kidded Greg for missing the elk. "I would have got him with my first shot."

He was gracious and replied, "That would be beginner's luck to bag an elk on your first day."

We became good friends during that hunt.

After hiking for a couple days in the high mountains of Colorado, carrying hunting gear, and trying not to let elk see our movements, trying not to make noise (which is almost impossible with dry leaves lying everywhere), or let our scent be caught down-wind, I decided to spend one morning near camp by myself under a tree with low over-hanging branches surrounded by brush. I had seen a hunter there the day before, sitting on a log. This spot was downhill 100 yards from the top of the bowl with grasses out in the center and trees lining both sides of the slopes.

There I sat in the quiet for about 45 minutes. Then I heard something behind me moving slowly, first crackling a branch and then leaves every now and then. It wasn't a branch falling off a tree, of that I was sure. I was nervous not knowing what it was, as the sounds kept moving closer. Could it see me, smell me, or hear my breathing? Could it be something other than an elk or deer? Perhaps a bear, or even a mountain lion? I dared not move to take a look and give my position away. After about 15 more minutes it came into my left peripheral vision—a hunter wearing orange. He nodded toward me and I replied the same. I was relieved yet disappointed. The hunter continued on his path across the meadow and disappeared out of my sight.

A half hour later, again I heard the breaking of small branches and crackling leaves behind me. This time it was to my right and I froze in place, gun off safety cradled in my arms, ready to shoot, hoping to see a bull elk.

About 50 feet away, out slowly stepped a magnificent buck which was up-wind from me and did not smell, hear, or see me. I did not have a deer license. He looked around, listened, and then slowly munched on the grasses as he meandered in a half circle around me about 50 feet away. A peaceful, gentle breeze was blowing. The buck was in his element. I thought how beautiful this creature was with slick shiny fur, fully buffed out muscles, antlers as large as any I've seen.

When he reached the edge of the grasses on my left he suddenly lifted his head and looked in my direction as he caught wind of my scent. The wind was circling around at that moment. He stared for maybe 30 seconds and saw no movement nor heard any sound from me. I thought he would continue into the trees but he lowered his head and continued to munch on grass. Turning in the opposite circular pattern, he fed on grass for another 15 minutes and disappeared again on my right where he first entered the meadow. I thought right then, if mine was a deer license, I would not shoot him. He was so beautiful. I found myself hoping he would live through the hunting season.

The next day I went to the bottom of the bowl where I sat on a huge boulder overlooking the opening that led to the bowl. It was an excellent vantage point to see anything pass through the lowest part the valley. I finally got tired of sitting on the boulder, neither seeing nor hearing anything except one other hunter. I wanted to be a real hunter by tracking my elk. I thought tracking would help me concentrate on my movements. Aspens lined the road where I started up the slope, being as quiet as possible, taking one step every ten to twenty seconds.

I was moving very slowly up the road about 100 yards when, out of the corner of my left eye, about 30 feet away, a movement captured my attention. I froze. There lying in grass was a full grown buck, which had been watching me for the last 50 yards. He had slightly moved his antlers.

We looked at each other.

I decided to just keep going up the road slowly. As I passed him and the road turned a little to my left about 25 feet away, the buck stood and I watched him cross the road and meander down the slope. It could have been the same buck I had seen the day before.

It was quite an eye opener experience to be right next to

him and not even see him. If he had not moved I no doubt would never have seen him.

After that first day, I never got close enough again to an elk—during hunting season—to shoot one. I learned a new respect for nature, though. The wild animals' ability to see, hear, and smell danger is far superior to ours.

The experience of being so close to the majestic buck, sharing that space and moment with him, truly felt like a privilege. I guess I would call that "beginner's luck"—or a blessing from God.

I really enjoyed the hunt!

ENCOUNTERS OF WONDER

poems by Mary Harwell Sayler

ZEBRA STRIPES ABBREVIATED—

In a butterfly wing…

The mango head of a condor
—orange-pink
as Pacific sunsets…

The spokes of an umbrella
folding and unfolding the arms
of a bat in a cavern,
dark, damp, and deep.

What wonder! What beauty!
What wit You have written
into creation, O Creator God.

THE OWL DID NOT
CALL MY NAME BUT—

Flew by without a sound—
barely above the ground—before
    landing on a lower branch
    of the cedar we call "Leb,"

Then turning its back to me,
to display grey-brown feathers
   dappled in white to match
   the tree's catch of sun.

The owl still did not call
nor ask the important question:
   Who? Who?
But I know, Lord, it's You—
The One Who truly knows
   my name.

EVEN IF THE HAWK KILLS—

Colorful songbirds in our yard,
I praise You for the birds of prey,
   who lift us as they soar
   majestically.

And even if the coral snake
hides poison beneath our shed,
I praise You for designing such
   flamboyant
   bands of beauty.

And though the bougainvillea stabs
with its long thorns, I praise You
for reminders of Your crown
   and the beautiful red flowers
   bleeding on the lawn.

ANIMALS IN THE WILDFIRE

by Catherine Lawton

W atching reports of the disastrous Tubbs fire in the Santa Rosa, California area (our old hometown), in the fall of 2018, our first thoughts were for the people and their homes. Then I began to wonder about the pets, livestock, and wildlife of the area.

My sister, Beverly, who lives there, went to bed unsuspecting, then a few hours later woke with a neighbor pounding on her door and yelling "fire." The neighbor later told her they had pounded and yelled a long time. Her dog's barking finally woke her. She hadn't heard the police earlier who drove through the neighborhood with a bull horn telling everyone to get out *now*!

I thank God for Bev's dog barking and waking her up.

A friend was living alone in a house on the edge of the city. From her back bedroom, she didn't hear the first responders ring her doorbell, and they assumed no one was home. What finally woke her was an annoying sound of scratching on the wood siding of the house outside her bedroom. She got up and looked out the window and saw racoons desperately trying to find shelter to get away from … fire! Fire just outside! The barn had already burned. She got out just in time but lost everything.

Did God encourage those raccoons to scratch there and wake her up?

Another friend lived high on a mountain road above Santa Rosa on a ranch where he and my son used to go exploring when they were boys. From his high vantage point this friend could see the fire moving closer. He chose to stay up there, alone, and worked hard through the night and day to save his home and some nearby structures as well. As he worked at the edge of the fire in the darkness, he said he felt wild animals brushing against him as they fled the burning areas. But he didn't stop and neither did they.

The Forestry Department urged people, who lived near, but not in, the wildfire areas, to bring their domestic animals indoors at night and let the wild ones pass through. "Please put out buckets of water for them—they are scared, exhausted, and have also lost their homes—they need to refuel."

One person had left buckets of water out for the deer and birds that came by her front yard. When she was allowed to return briefly to her home she found a dozen turkey vultures and other birds resting on her lawn together. They looked exhausted, so much so that they didn't even move when she went up to her door, she said.

Many people had to flee within minutes and had no time to find their cats. One woman said she was surprised that "leaving my cat was almost the thing that hit me the hardest" about the wildfire.

Some dogs panicked and ran, and their owners had to evacuate and flee the flames without them. One report said someone tried to get their horses into a trailer, but the frightened horses refused; so the people had to leave their horses.

Evacuees posted online such announcements as:

- "We are looking for two donkeys that we had to leave. Do you know their whereabouts?"

- "Lost Dog: While her family was evacuating, she

jumped out of their truck. They love this dog so much and are devastated."

• "54 horses in dire need of transportation off a ranch."

• "Cat found hiding under car. Whiskers burnt but she's okay."

• "Our husky slipped out of her collar while we were evacuating and ran off. Heartbroken."

Many dogs and cats, and well as horses and other animals were lost and frightened, with burnt feet and ears and singed whiskers. Clinics were set up, volunteers worked to treat them and comfort them, and to reunite people with their animals.

The re-uniting of people and animals brought mutual comfort and joy.

REMINDER THAT GOD IS WITH US

a poem by Sarah Suzanne Noble

IN THE GREY

In the grey
  I see a red bird
A cardinal
  Roosting on chair
He stares
  Right in my eye
As I stretch
  As my muscles ache
He stares
  The rain drops fall
In April
  A snowstorm a day ago
He stares
  Buds limp from cold
Petals on floor
  God, you stare
You see me in the grey
  In waiting
Thank you for the bird
  That stares
A reminder that you
  Are everywhere
And at the same time
  With me in grey
Hope for the day

WILD OBSERVATIONS

by Susan Roberts

THE RABBIT AND BEANS

It was bean planting time. I was stooping over the raised bed, placing bedding plants in holes, when a Cottontail Rabbit came within a few feet of me. Explaining garden etiquette, I patiently informed him my bean plants were not his to nibble, but he could enjoy the grass or other delectables in my yard that would not be destroyed by his feasting. He proceeded, however, to chomp on my baby bean plants right in front of me! I promptly shooed this critter from my garden!

God has set out rules for us too. David outlined the benefits of God's laws in Psalm 19. They revive us, make us wise, and show us truth about who God is. They warn us of pitfalls. Keeping them brings us great reward and blessing.

WHO'S CALLING?

An eerie howl pierced the quiet of the evening. My husband and I looked at each other and said simultaneously, "What was that?" We heard a sound like a scream or a wail. A little research showed us that it was a Fox call. Yes, we now know what the Fox says. Our research also showed that each family of Foxes has a distinct voice, recognizable by the others. Varying tones represent their communication, usually initiated by the mom. She calls them to dinner, she "interrogates" them to see where they are and what they are doing, and she alerts them to danger.

When I was growing up in the days before cell phones, our neighborhood moms had varied calls too. My mom used a large bell, another had a whistle, and a third a horn. We were to stay within range and pay attention. When we heard our call, we were to drop what we were doing and run home.

God calls us as well, and we should be attentive to his voice. Listen to what God is calling you to do.

UNSTUCK

We had some excitement at our house while our daughter and her family were visiting recently. Our young grandson came running up from the basement screaming. His family had been playing soccer downstairs and discovered that a Prairie Dog had fallen into the window well. We tried to remove him, but the more we tugged, the more he buried himself in the dirt with only his butt and tail showing. I finally got a garden trowel and dug through the hard dirt to unearth enough of him so we could grab him and pull him out. He was not happy. I'm sure he was very scared with all the commotion, yelling, and yanking. We had to do it for his own good or he would've died. We released him into the backyard, and hopefully he found his way back to his colony. Perhaps he learned his lesson and will stay away from houses in the future.

Like the Prairie Dog, we get ourselves into fixes and find we are stuck in an unhealthy relationship, lifestyle, or occupation. Though we might not realize it at the time, we desperately need to cooperate with God who desires to help and rescue us.

THE BIRDS

They swooped in a perfect V formation. Their white feathers flashed in the sunlight. The American White Pelicans were back. They migrate to our area each spring. We love to watch them fly in formation, floating and banking in unison, and gliding in gracefully to land on the lake. We are sad to see them leave in the fall.

A friend sent us a link to a YouTube video of thousands of starlings flying in unison, making exquisite patterns in the sky. The video explained these flight patterns are called murmerations, and scientists aren't sure why they happen; but they are beautiful.

One time we saw nearby trees filled with noisy birds. They didn't fly with grace and unity. Startled, they took to the air in mass confusion. What a haphazard swarm compared to the beauty of unity.

When Christians come together to work in unison, it is also beautiful. As one body, we can move together to create something wonderful, reflecting the Son.

REFLECTIONS

There wasn't even a ripple. The wind was still and the pond was as smooth as glass. Mountains, trees, sky and clouds reflected on the quiet water. A wood duck perched on a tree stump, sitting as motionless as the pool below, his image mirrored on the surface. A breeze came up and his feathers ruffled as his image disappeared from the broken waters. Off he flew, as if the disturbance had reminded him of places he needed to visit.

When we are quiet and receptive, we can hear God's voice, receive his prompting and be renewed in our inner being.

THE CHASE
It Happened On Londonberry Street

by Catherine Lawton

For twenty-five years we lived in an older neighbor-hood in an unincorporated area of small ranch-style houses on half acre lots, with many trees, including tall Redwoods, and with a creek running nearby, beyond which rose hills.

I loved taking walks through this neighborhood with its many flowers and greenery. Almost every neighbor had a cat or a dog or two, and you never knew what wildlife would appear, wandering into the neighborhood from the woodsy creek area.

One evening I was meditatively walking along London-berry Street, the meandering road along which houses were built whose backyards bordered Mark West Creek.

But suddenly I was awakened from my reverie by a mule deer running—right toward me! The deer seemed to be running for its life. Before it reached me (*phew!*) it veered into the space between two houses and disappeared, toward the creek behind.

Then, just as suddenly, a large dog came running straight toward me on the road. This was a little unnerving; but the dog, also, veered to its left, between the houses, and headed toward the creek.

My attention was quickly drawn back to the road straight ahead of me, because a man was then running toward me, panting, and breathlessly calling, "Have you seen a dog chasing a deer?"

"Yes. They both went that way." I pointed.

With a quick "Thanks!" he also veered to my right and ran past the house toward the creek.

I assume the deer evaded the dog, as wild creatures usually do. And I'm sure the man got his dog back and probably was more watchful after that. I'm sure the dog had a great time.

Smiling, I turned left onto my street and walked the last block home, my heart lifted. Whatever problem about which I had been cogitating earlier, had dissipated for now.

IT'S A BEAR!

by Catherine Lawton

Living all my life in California and Colorado and going camping in the Sierras, Cascades, and Coast Ranges, as well as the Rocky Mountains, I have had my share of bear encounters.

The first ones happened when I was about nine or ten years old. My parents and their friends, who also were in pastoral ministry and also had two little girls, decided to get away from the stresses of daily ministry work and go camping in the nearby mountains for a couple of nights. From our small, neighboring towns in the San Joaquin Valley, driving up to King's Canyon National Park provided a close, convenient, and cheap getaway.

Not to worry that we couldn't afford to rent a cabin and didn't own RVs or tents. No problem. The campsite had plenty of room for the four adults to sleep on the ground and the girls to sleep in the cars. We four girls had a great time climbing on rocks, running down paths, and sipping cocoa by the campfire. Our dads went fishing. Our moms cooked and tried to keep us tidy and within hearing range. Everyone enjoyed conversation.

After we girls were settled in with sleeping bags and blankets on the bench seats of our old cars, the adults sat talking as night fell deeper and stars shone brighter. No one thought to take the bag of trash to the camp garbage receptacle. In the morning, the trash had been scattered around and rummaged through, no doubt by the pesky raccoons.

Sometime during the second night the adults awoke to the sound of scratching and rummaging and assumed it was the raccoons again. Not wanting to acknowledge it and bring everyone wide awake, they each lay there listening and waiting for the raccoons to finish and leave. For some reason my mother decided to sit up and look. When she did, she let out a yell, "It's a bear!"

Meanwhile I had awakened and sat up to peer out the car window at the sleeping-bagged adults. What I saw was a small black bear, startled by Mother's outburst, running across the campsite—straight at my mother! My heart raced and my eyes grew wide. But the bear just jumped over Mother's sleeping bag and made its escape into the woods.

About a year or two later, my family was again camping—this time high in Yosemite National Park, and with a large, family-size tent. When we set up camp a ranger informed us that bears had been visiting the campgound in recent days. People locked their food items into metal coolers.

My mother, father, sister, and I were asleep on our cots when, in the middle of the night, loud banging sounds woke us. Voices called out, and the banging kept on, close by, sounding like something heavy was being thrown around just outside our tent. Daddy shone his flashlight out the tent flap.

"It's a bear. It has someone's ice chest." It was a determined bear. And as the racket continued, I felt sure it would rip up our tent next and find us tasty humans inside. I trembled from fear so violently that my cot was shaking. My parents tried to calm me down by telling me that the bears didn't want to get the people, just their food. But logic didn't help. I wasn't reassured and I couldn't stop shaking. At that moment I pictured the devil, not as a roaring lion* but as a raging bear, intent on my destruction in the dark.

I guess that bear finally succeeded and got the food out of the chest, and finally lumbered away, fatter and even more clever at outsmarting people.

The next day, the rangers showed us a heavy metal drum used for trapping nuisance bears. Far inside of the drum they had placed an open can of tuna, a favorite of the bears. The trap looked very strong and the rangers assured us it would work. Later in the day, word reached us that last night's bear had been caught in the trap and would be relocated, released deeper in the wilderness.

That childhood experience left me with a mental picture of the courageous rangers with a trap strong enough to capture a powerful bear.

I have since enjoyed sightings of black bears from a distance, like the time my husband and I saw a mother bear and three cubs ambling over the rocks beside Bear Lake Road in Rocky Mountain National Park.

People are more educated now to respect wildlife, to not feed or tantalize bears by leaving food items where they can get to them.

And I have learned not to feed fearful thoughts, not to let them overcome me, but to trap them so to speak, and to release them far away from my mind and heart.

"We take captive every thought ..." 2 Cor. 10:5

---

*See I Peter 5:8

LOVE THAT WILL NOT ...

a poem by Alice Scott-Ferguson

We, and every bird that sings,
every blade that brings forth fruit,
every worm that burrows in the ground
connected, founded in the desire
of universal intelligence
called the Christ—
He who loved all into sentience
and proclaimed it sacred and good,
tuning the benevolent beating of our hearts,
setting the rhythm of every breath,
synchronizing every life force to start
and stay, to adapt in awesome array.
All creation retains the imprimatur of Love,
of a sapience greater than our limitations,
who conducts the orchestra of miraculous grace
in wild beauty of wilderness and restless seas.
May we become aware, and face-to-face
with one another, animal, mountain and meadow
behold the wonder of our world hung in space,
the value and worth of the broken and bent.
And with reverent, tender compassion
love all with the same passion that sent the first cell
into life-pulsing perpetuity; the offspring of divinity,
of love that will not let go.

ABOUT ...

The Compiler

Catherine Lawton is poet, writer, and editor who founded Cladach Publishing in 1999. She enjoys giving opportunities to talented authors, producing books that show our loving God at work in our world and people working with God, for good. In her own writings, Catherine explores facets of how we relate mutually with God, nature, and each other. Much of her inspiration comes on mountain trails and meadows, in gardens and gatherings, and along rivers and salty shores. She is a regular contributor to the Godspace Light blog as well as her own at https://cladach.com/blog/. Books she has authored include:

> *Face to Face: A Novel*
> *No More Fear: From Killing Field to Harvest Fields* (as told to)
> *Journeys to Mother Love: Nine Women Tell Their Stories of*
>   *Forgiveness and Healing* (compilation)
> *Remembering Softly: A Life In Poems*
> *Glimpsing Glory: Poems of Living & Dying, Praying & Playing,*
>   *Belonging & Longing*

The Contributors

Marilyn Bay In addition to writing and editing agricultural publications, Marilyn operates Prairie Natural Lamb. She enjoys training horses and is a certified Colorado 4-H horse show judge and level rater. Marilyn has authored two Cladach titles:

> *Prairie Truth: A Novel*
> *All We Like Sheep: Lessons from the Sheepfold* (with Mildred Bay)

Mildred (Millie) Bay has raised sheep for decades in Northern Colorado. She has served with Gideons International, as a 4-H leader, and has had numerous articles published in local newspapers and the *Gideon Lamp*. She co-authored *All We Like Sheep: Lessons from the Sheepfold* with her daughter Marilyn Bay.

Susan Bulanda has worked as a Canine Search and Rescue trainer and handler in both the U.S. and Europe, a senior conformation judge for the United Kennel Club, a lecturer at Kutztown University in dog training and behavior consulting, and a private animal behavior consultant. Her many published books include two released by Cladach:

God's Creatures: A Biblical View of Animals
Faithful Friends: Holocaust Survivors' Stories of the Pets Who Gave Them Comfort, Suffered Alongside Them and Waited for Their Return

John Buzzard served in the U.S. Navy during Operation Desert Storm in 1991. He has resided in California, Montana, and Arizona. He writes westerns and historical fiction. Cladach released John's historical novel:

That Day By the Creek: A Novel About the Sand Creek Massacre of 1864

Beverly Coons is retired from a career as a seventh-grade English teacher. She lives in Santa Rosa, California, where she enjoys church activities, walking her dog, gardening, tea with friends, and horse riding. She journals daily and has had several stories published in *Sonoma County Horse Journal.*

G.H. Cummings (1924-2019) was an ordained minister in the Church of the Nazarene, a licensed counselor, and a writer. He grew up on a farm in St. Francis, Kansas, served with the U.S. Army in Korea, and pastored churches in Colorado, California, and Oregon. Later he had a private counseling practice in Idaho. He authored:

Making It In Marriage: It's Worth The Effort

Dennis Ellingson has served with the Salvation Army and pastored country churches. He developed expertise as an herbalist and has led plant walks in both Southern Oregon and Arizona. Cladach has released three of Dennis's books:

The Godly Grandparent: Living Faithfully and Influencing Your Grandchildren For Christ

God's Healing Herbs
God's Wild Herbs: Identifying and Using 121 Plants Found In the Wild

Kit Ellingson has served alongside her husband, Dennis, in ministry and community outreach. She co-authored *The Godly Grandparent* with her husband. Kit is a professional photographer.

Alice Scott-Ferguson is a native of the Shetland Islands of Scotland, who immigrated to the U.S. as a young woman. She is now retired in Arizona. She has written and taught Bible studies and produced prize-winning poetry. Cladach has released three of her books:

*Mothers Can't Be Everywhere But God Is: A Liberating Look
    At Motherhood*
Pausing In The Passing Places: Poems
Unpaused Poems: Real, Raw, Relevant

Jeanie Flierl lives in Colorado and writes fiction. Jeanie has been a business owner for many years and active in marriage ministry, teaching communication skills and speaking to groups. Cladach released Jeanie's first novel:

To Conquer A Mountain: A Novel

Gayle M. Irwin grew up in Iowa and now resides in Wyoming. Gayle is a journalist and a conservation and humane educator. She is the author of many books including the Cladach title:

Walking In Trust: Lessons Learned With My Blind Dog

Susan Elaine Jenkins lived in China for nearly twenty years, teaching the performing arts in international schools. She now resides in California, her home state, where she continues to work in the field of education. Her memoir was released by Cladach:

Scandalon: Running From Shame & Finding God's Scandalous Love

Larry Lawton is the finance and sales director at Cladach Publishing. He is retired from a career in accounting. His writing experience is mainly in the area of documentation, procedures, and policies. A native of Northern California, he enjoys living in Colorado, where he plays basketball, gardens, and explores the mountains.

Janyne McConnaughey is retired from a forty-year career in education. Janyne now is redeeming her story of trauma by helping others to understand and heal from childhood trauma. She currently resides in Seattle. She serves on the Board of Directors of the Attachment & Trauma Network, Inc, and continues to speak and write books, three of which are memoirs published by Cladach:

Brave: A Personal Story of Healing Childhood Trauma
Jeanie's Brave Childhood: Behavior and Healing through the Lens of Attachment and Trauma
A Brave Life: Survival, Resilience, Faith & Hope After Childhood Trauma

Donna Marie Merritt is a poet and educator who lives in Connecticut and works as a school librarian. She is the author of seven books of poetry for adults and seventeen books for children. Cladach released her poetry collection:

Bible Poems For Reflection and Response

Sarah Suzanne Noble is a poet, photographer, and artist living and creating in Chicago. She practiced architecture and design for several years. Sarah is involved in several ministries, including marriage mentoring and crisis support. Cladach released her poetry collection:

I Cry Unto You O Lord: Poems of Lament

Carol O'Casey writes from her background as a field biologist, teacher, and ministry leader. She lives in Oregon. She has taught science to college students and also to sixth graders. Carol's passion is expounding the wonders tucked in God's wilds. She is the author of the Cladach title:

Unwrapping Wonder: Finding Hope In the Gift of Nature

Judith Galblum Pex was born in Washington, D.C. She and her husband, John, live in Eilat, Israel, where they run The Shelter Hostel, a guest house for travelers from all over the world. Judy enjoys hiking and camping in the mountains around Eilat, snorkeling in the Red Sea, traveling and photography. Judy has authored three Cladach titles:
Walk the Land: A Journey On Foot Through Israel
A People Tall and Smooth: Stories of Escape From Sudan To Israel
Come, Stay, Celebrate!: The Story of the Shelter Hostel In Eilat, Israel

Susan Roberts grew up in Massachusetts then attended college in Illinois, then lived in many places as a military wife. Susan worked twenty years as a school secretary. She writes a bi-weekly devotional, "God Sightings." She is the author of two books including the Cladach title:
Everywhere I Look, God Is There: 180 Daily Devotional Discoveries

Mary Harwell Sayler has placed 28 books in all genres with Christian and educational publishers. Over 2,000 of her poems, articles, devotionals, and children's stories have appeared in print and online periodicals. She regularly blogs on Bible topics and poetry. Cladach released her poetry collection:
PRAISE! Poems

Nancy Swihart has served as Professor of English and Department Head of General Studies at Manhattan Christian College in Kansas; editor and writer for National Center for Fathering; speaker at various women's retreats and conferences; and founding member, with her husband, Jud, of Wellspring, Inc. She is the author of a memoir published by Cladach:
On Kitten Creek: Searching For the Sacred

ACKNOWLEDGEMENTS

p. 5 and p. 12: Quotes by Elizabeth Theokritoff and reference to Maximus the Confessor are from the book, *Living In God's Creation: Orthodox Perspectives On Ecology* (St Vladimir's Seminary Press, 2009).

p. 13: John Stott is quoted from "Christians and Animals," *Christianity Today* (February 10, 1978).

p. 13: Charles Camosy is quoted from: https://www.ncronline.org/news/earthbeat/gods-plan-animals-hot-topic-theology-we-can-all-understand

p. 52: "Bogar" by Kathy Rubin first appeared in *Faithful Friends* by Susan Bulanda (Cladach, 2011).

p. 62: The poem "Three" first appeared in the poetry collection *Pausing In the Passing Places* by Alice Scott-Ferguson (Cladach, 2018).

p. 87: Lines of the 9th-century poem are extracted from the complete translated poem quoted by Esther De Waal in *Every Earthly Blessing: Rediscovering the Celtic Tradition* (Morehouse, 1999).

p. 100: "The Cat We Left Behind" by Jacob Stern first appeared in *Faithful Friends* by Susan Bulanda (Cladach, 2011) under the title "The Cat."

p. 103: Wendell Berry quoted from his book titled *Bringing it to the Table: On Farming and Food* (Counterpoint, 2009).

p. 105: "My 'Hey, Sheep'" is excerpted from *On Kitten Creek* by Nancy Swihart (Cladach, 2017).

p.113: "Dust Bowl Days" is excerpted and published posthumously from a self-published memoir, *This Man's Family*.

p. 120: "What Charlene Taught Me" is excerpted from *All We Like Sheep* by Mildred Bay and Marilyn Bay (Cladach, 2015).

p. 124: "Netta and the Sheep Pony" is excerpted from *All We Like Sheep* by Mildred Bay and Marilyn Bay (Cladach, 2015).

p. 127: "Run To Safety!" is excerpted from *All We Like Sheep* by Mildred Bay and Marilyn Bay (Cladach, 2015).

p. 130: "Freckles: The Faithful Farm Dog" is excerpted from *All We Like Sheep* by Mildred Bay and Marilyn Bay (Cladach, 2015).

p. 144: Hedgehog photo © Can Stock Photo / antpkr.
Cricket in cage photo © IvanWalsh from Shanghai, China, via Wikimedia Commons. (All other photos in the book provided compliments of the individuals identified in the captions.)

p. 147: "Grace Sings on Cricket Wings" is excerpted from *Unwrapping Wonder* by Carol O'Casey (Cladach, 2013).

p. 159: "Toads and Salamanders" by Catherine Lawton first appeared under the title "Treasures of Darkness: Holy Stillness" at https://godspacelight.com/2021/03/27/treasures-of-darkness-holy-stillness/

p. 168: "Honeybees" is condensed and adapted from an essay by Catherine Lawton entitled "Opening To God Through Prayer" that first appeared in the book, *Uncontrolling Love: Essays Exploring the Love of God,* edited by Baker, Coffin, Drurey, Kirksey, Michaels, and Ward (SacraSage, 2017).

p. 178: "Backyard Birds" poems first appeared in *Glimpsing Glory* by Catherine Lawton (Cladach, 2020).

p. 186: 'Encounters of Wonder" poems first appeared in *PRAISE! Poems* by Mary Harwell Sayler (Cladach, 2017).

p. 188: "Animals in the Wildfire" by Catherine Lawton first appeared as a blog post at https://cladach.com/blog/.

p. 192: "Wild Observations" are excerpted from *Everywhere I Look, God Is There* by Susan Roberts (Cladach, 2016).

p. 201: "Love That Will Not" first appeared in *Unpaused Poems* by Alice Scott-Ferguson (Cladach, 2021).

CPSIA information can be obtained
at www.ICGtesting.com
Printed in the USA
FSHW011759040821
83629FS